Imaging Life
After Death

Imaging Life After Death

Love That Moves the Sun and Stars

Kathleen Fischer

Paulist Press
New York/Mahwah, N.J.

Cover image: Gogh, Vincent van (1853–1890) © Digital Image © The Museum of Modern Art/Licensed by SCALA/Art Resource, NY. The Starry Night. 1889. Oil on canvcas, 29 x 36 1/4". Acquired through the Lillie P. Bliss Bequest. (472. 1941) Location: The Museum of Modern Art, New York, NY, USA.

Scripture extracts are taken from the New Revised Standard Version, Copyright © 1989, by the Division of Christian Education of the National Council of the Churches of Christ in the United States of America and reprinted by permission of the publisher.

Cover design by Sharyn Banks
Book design by Lynn Else

Library of Congress Cataloging-in-Publication Data

Fischer, Kathleen, 1940–
    Imaging life after death : love that moves the sun and stars / Kathleen Fischer.
      p.   cm.
    Includes bibliographical references.
    ISBN 0-8091-4244-9 (alk. paper)
    1. Future life—Christianity. I. Title.

BT903.F57 2004
236'.2—dc22

2004007374

Published by Paulist Press
997 Macarthur Boulevard
Mahwah, New Jersey 07430

www.paulistpress.com

Printed and bound in Canada

Contents

Acknowledgments

*T*he Publisher gratefully acknowledges use of the following:

Lines from "In Whom We Live and Move and Have Our Being" and "Primary Wonder" by Denise Levertov, from *Sands of the Well*. Copyright © 1996 by Denise Levertov. Reprinted by permission of New Directions Publishing Corp. and Bloodaxe Books.

Lines from Jelaluddin Rumi, "Say Yes Quickly" from *Open Secret: Versions of Rumi*, translated by John Moyne and Coleman Barks. Copyright © 1984 by John Moyne and Coleman Barks. Reprinted by arrangement with Shambhala Publications, Inc., Boston, www.shambhala.com.

"Merger Poem" by Judy Chicago. Copyright © 1979 by Judy Chicago. Reprinted by permission of Through the Flower.

Lines from "Sunrise" by Mary Oliver, from *Dream Work*. Copyright © 1986 by Mary Oliver. Used by permission of Grove/Atlantic, Inc. Lines from *The Leaf and the Cloud* by Mary Oliver. Copyright © 2000 by Mary Oliver. Reprinted by permission of Perseus Books Publishers, a member of Perseus Books, L.L.C.

Lines from "Cover Photograph," from *Fields of Praise: New and Selected Poems* by Marilyn Nelson. Copyright © 1997 by Marilyn Nelson. Reprinted by permission of Louisiana State University Press.

Psalm 16 and four lines from Psalm 23, from *A Book of Psalms: Selected and Adapted from the Hebrew* by Stephen Mitchell. Copyright © 1993 by Stephen Mitchell. Reprinted by permission of HarperCollins Publishers, Inc.

"Into the Bright Immensities" by Rita Rainsford Rouner, from *If I Should Die*, edited by Leroy Rouner. Copyright © 2001 by

Preface

decided to write this book after years of walking with others as they grieved the loss of someone close to them, or made their own journey into death. They made me aware of how significant the subject of life after death suddenly becomes. At these times, the topic takes on immediacy, like a project continually postponed to a future date and now suddenly due.

There are those who then find that traditional teachings on the afterlife still speak to them. But others, though they want to believe, can no longer relate to the images that once sustained their hope. They find little meaning in familiar passages of scripture or lines from a creed, in statements about the gates of heaven or the fires of hell. They ask me if I still believe in these realities. Their questions become very practical, and can be grouped under three general headings: What survives death? Do relationships continue beyond death? How does life now relate to life then?

While the book's central issues and its structure come from these conversations, my own background shapes the way I approach them. Early in my doctoral work in religious studies I learned what it is like to have traditional beliefs bump up against a contemporary view of the world. I began graduate courses confident of the classical theology I had so diligently learned. But soon I was roaming in a universe more complex and changing than any I had known before, the world of thinkers like Teilhard de Chardin and Alfred North Whitehead. It was both frightening and exhilarating. Ultimately it enabled me to live with greater integrity, as I discovered that even the practice of prayer made more sense in this new vision so fundamentally grounded in relationships and mutual influence.

In the years since I left graduate school, science has revealed a universe even more vast and mysterious. And it has also reinforced the idea that we can know only the material, the things we can observe and measure. In such a cosmos, what can it mean to believe in life after death? My reflections on the afterlife are situated within this new cosmic story, and I trust that faith will again be enriched by the insights and challenges this story offers.

While science opens up new perspectives, it also has limits. There are important dimensions of human experience and concern that elude its grasp. Only a rich array of disciplines—science, scripture, poetry, literature, story, prayer—can do justice to some very important topics, life after death among them. The language and modes of the imagination are especially fruitful here. Even the imaginative speech of poetry, metaphor, and analogy falls short, but it can at least suggest realities that span body and spirit and connect this life with the next. Words of the imagination can also better express paradoxes like decay and new life, and contradictions like horror and beauty. That is why I build many of my chapters around different images for the afterlife: seeds and butterflies, fire and light.

Mystics and prophets from many of the world's religious traditions attest to life after death. Taken all together, their witness is quite compelling. Though my own background is Christian, I have learned from these other religions, and try to show the broad basis for the human belief in promise and redemption. My hope is that this overview of the topic will stimulate further conversation among those of different spiritual traditions, as well as those who embrace no such affiliations.

Even with these testimonies across time, the fact remains that we have no direct knowledge of the beyond. We have only hints and pointers from this-worldly experiences. The full reality remains shrouded in mystery. Talk of the afterlife is, like talk of God, partial and suggestive.

The lives of ordinary persons are an important source of information regarding life after death. Though most people do not consider themselves experts in matters of theology, they do live with the Mystery. And so I show how everyday experiences—humor, hope, beauty, forgiveness, memory, and love—contain intimations of eternity. We need to listen, as well, to accounts of near-death experiences and stories of the presence of loved ones who have died.

There are those who fear that a focus on life beyond death will distract us from the work necessary to preserve our fragile planet and bring about justice in this world. But when rightly understood, belief in an afterlife does not erode care of the Earth, nor divert determination to work for change. For me, in fact, it increases concern for the universe and sustains the courage we need to oppose all forms of oppression.

Although topics like heaven and hell are usually placed in the category of *last things*, they really belong to our present, ordinary days. What we were taught to anticipate after death is not something tacked on to existence at the last minute, but the fulfillment of what we are now living. Eternal life is already in the making. In a way, then, this book about life after death is a book of contemporary spirituality as well, an invitation to contemplation and the good life—justice, mercy, love, and care for all creation. It reflects the holistic vision that informs my work as a therapist, spiritual director, and teacher.

I hope it will be helpful to those who are dying or grieving the loss of a loved one, as well as to those who work with them in any way. It is also intended for anyone who wants to explore the topic, either alone or with others. It is designed so that it can be easily used in discussion groups.

Some approaches to the question will appeal to you more than others. For this reason, the section "Notes and Further Reading" not only identifies the sources of my own thinking, but also provides resources for pursuing different issues in greater depth. Since belief about life after death is not simply a theoretical matter, but one of the most important questions we face alone and together, I include a chapter on walking with the dying, and end each chapter with suggestions for prayer and reflection. Finally, when quoting individuals I have spoken with, I have changed identifying information to protect their privacy.

Part I

What Survives Death?

1. Invisible Realities

here is an ancient tale in which several disciples approach their Master, full of questions about God.

Said the Master, "God is the Unknown
and the Unknowable. Every statement made
about Him, every answer to your questions,
is a distortion of the Truth."

The disciples were bewildered. "Then
why do you speak about Him at all?"

"Why does the bird sing?" said the
Master.

In attempting to depict the afterlife, we struggle with the same limits encountered in talking about God. Language is inadequate. There is so much that is not known. Yet human beings cannot keep from asking the question, Is there something more? It arises from who we are, like the song of the bird.

Talk of an afterlife is especially hard today because of widespread belief that only matter or the physical, as science defines it, is real. Some forms of this scientific materialism reduce reality even more by declaring that only the smallest isolated elements

3

are real. Since materialism is pervasive in modern culture, the burden of proof is on anyone who affirms the existence of the spiritual, or professes to believe in an invisible God. Declaring that there is an afterlife seems a bit foolish, like being caught wearing hopelessly outdated clothes. But it is possible to respect the scientific method and at the same time to recognize its limitations. A complete picture of life includes not only what can be objectively weighed and measured, but also a sacred reality not so clearly seen.

More Than Meets the Eye

There are many ways of knowing. Knowledge of God and an afterlife requires a different mode of perception than the scientific. I like the analogy the philosopher Mary Midgley uses for how we perceive reality. She compares human life to an enormous ill-lit aquarium. We can never see it fully from above, but must peer through small windows at various locations around it. Scientific windows are just one important kind. Fish and other aquarium dwellers continually dart away from particular windows, move in and out among rocks and weeds, or swim to other areas where we cannot see them. Then they reappear in locations where different lighting makes them easier to recognize. Midgley believes that long experience, as well as quick dashing between windows, improves our skill at tracking. However, if we refuse to synthesize the data from certain windows, we have only a partial picture. Why, she asks, should unbelief rather than belief be the best response to all the knowledge we are able to gather?

Many scientists themselves affirm the existence of more than they can see. Russell Stannard, head of the physics department at the Open University in London, describes how his own field of high-energy nuclear physics exemplifies this. He researches the behavior of subatomic particles too small to be seen directly. Because they are invisible, it is necessary to draw inferences from observing their effects. The particles usually leave a trail—like a string of tiny bubbles in a transparent liquid—marking where they have been. As these subatomic particles collide with each other, or spontaneously disintegrate, they create characteristic patterns that mark the path they followed.

Paul Davies, professor of mathematical physics at the University of Adelaide in Australia, makes a similar point. He notes that we cannot kick, see, or smell everything we trust, as though it were some kind of concrete block. Atoms are too tiny to see or touch directly. The same is true of quantum fields, which are indistinct configurations of invisible energy. Davies believes modes of knowing that are different from the scientific apply to many things in ordinary life: music, mathematics, information, thoughts, and emotions.

This way of knowing the invisible from the effects it produces is not so unlike the way each of the major religious traditions judges genuine religious experience. Authentic relationship with the Holy leaves a trail. It is a path marked by compassion. As the prophet Muhammad said, "Do you love your Creator? Love your fellow beings first." There is, in fact, quite widespread agreement about how genuine experiences of the Transcendent are validated. The test is the long-term effects in a person's life. Matthew's Gospel sums it up: "You will know them by their fruits" (7:16). Mystics of every tradition caution us not to focus on secondary matters, like visions or blissful feelings, but on how contact with the divine transforms a person's life. During years of doing spiritual direction, I learned to listen on two levels as people describe their prayer. I tune one ear to the prayer account, the other to how the person's life is going. Many people find prayer dark and awash in distractions, yielding little sense of God's presence. As in nature, there are deserts, spare landscapes, and barren plains. This is especially true in times of physical or mental illness. It is in our lives that we attest to a relationship with the Holy.

Religious experiences do not appear on demand and according to our measure of reality; there are surprises, disappointments, the expanding of horizons. Moments of more intense union generally occur within an ongoing relationship with the Transcendent. They are given to us, not produced by us. Over time they lead to greater freedom, peace, and love. They do not answer many questions, nor set aside all doubts. As an older friend often says to me: "Of course I have doubts. Faith is just that, *faith*." Ever aware of the limits of human knowing, persons whose religious experience is genuine do not claim to know much about the Mystery. They are the first to insist that their experience is completely inadequate to who God is. As the poet T. S. Eliot reminds us, we have here only "hints and guesses."

It will be helpful to keep these criteria in mind when we talk in later chapters about relationships between the living and dead. As we will see, the kind of presence that links heaven and earth has similar characteristics, since it is the way our lives are joined in God.

Are We Fooling Ourselves?

If we profess to believe in an afterlife, we not only risk being behind the times, we might also be thought crazy. When a client describes a friend's conversations with his wife who died several months ago, she asks: "Is he hallucinating?" Another tells me about a sense she had of God's presence while hiking the Pacific Coast Trail: "I didn't tell my friends, though, because I didn't want them to think I was crazy." The fear is that these experiences are illusory.

There are many reasons for this equating of religious belief with illusion, but surely one of the most powerful is the influence of Sigmund Freud, the Austrian psychoanalyst whose life spanned the late nineteenth and early twentieth centuries. Freud declared that religious belief arises from wish fulfillment. We long for something and then assure ourselves that it is real. We fear death and want life to continue, so we convince ourselves that there is an afterlife. Freud believed this yearning for spiritual union is actually an unconscious desire to escape the disappointments of life and return to the blissful unity we knew as infants. Although his theories stemmed from his own life and convictions, rather than research regarding actual religious experience, they are still entrenched in Western culture.

According to Freud, we need to grow up, get beyond such comforting illusions, and face the harsh realities of life. But belief in an afterlife does not protect us from terrible grief when a loved one dies, nor shield us from fear of death. Further, Freud ignored the way religion not only comforts, but also challenges, and he seemed unaware of the positive beauty and power of many spiritual experiences. Research in fact shows that individuals who have genuine spiritual experiences enjoy better psychological health than people in general. They have improved interpersonal relationships, higher self-esteem, lower levels of anxiety, clearer self-identity, increased concern for others, and a more positive overall outlook on life.

Finally, it is obvious that religion has no corner on illusion and bias. Anything can be distorted or misused—art, information, science, technology, money, ideas, and love. States of mind marked by hallucinations and delusions do, of course, occur. They are accompanied by other factors that indicate a major mental illness or the presence of side effects from medications or sickness. They are not confined to the religious realm, but can cover the whole span of human experience. Certain illnesses, such as schizophrenia and bipolar disorder, can trigger voices, visions, or hallucinations that focus at times on the spiritual. It is imperative that professionals diagnose and treat these conditions. But it is equally important that we do not use these diagnostic terms as derogatory labels for what goes beyond our definition of the real, thereby eliminating even the possibility of healthy religious experience.

Restricting reality to the material and equating religion with illusion account for some of the difficulties we have in trying to talk about the afterlife. Others result from how we think about God.

Locating and Describing God

In the year 1519, the Portuguese navigator Ferdinand Magellan set sail from Spain to find a western passage to the Spice Islands in Indonesia. On the long and disastrous voyage, Magellan was killed and two of his ships were destroyed. But one, the *Victoria*, eventually circled the world.

At journey's end, a seemingly trivial disagreement occurred. Throughout the ship's absence of nearly three years, each day's write-up had been scrupulously dated in the ship's log. According to these records, it was Wednesday, July 9, 1522, when the ship arrived at the Cape Verde Islands. But the Portuguese inhabitants said that it was Thursday, July 10. The navigators thought the Portuguese were wrong, and sailed on to Sanlucar, certain it was now Saturday, September 6. The Spaniards who greeted them there insisted it was Sunday, September 7. The explorers had to face the fact that somehow they had dropped twenty-four hours from the calendar.

Scientists later solved the riddle. Copernicus was right. Rolling eastward, the Earth completes a full circle every day. Sailing westward against that rotation, Magellan's navigators gained precisely twenty-four hours as they traveled a full circle. The Earth is round, not flat. Furthermore, it is revolving on its own axis. This leads to the shocking conclusion that the world is not the center of the universe. Moreover, if the Earth is revolving daily, then heaven and hell cannot be found in their traditional locations above and beneath the Earth. Skepticism about their existence began to grow. It has continued since, as information about the universe expands beyond anything medieval faith could ever have imagined.

But language about God, heaven, and hell has not stood still during these five centuries. It is no longer bound to categories of *above* and *below*. There are other ways to express God's distance and closeness, and other maps for heaven and hell. The one that informs much contemporary thinking about the afterlife is the view that the cosmos dwells within God, but God is not limited to the cosmos. Not only is God present in everything, all things are also simultaneously held within God. Thus the whole universe is a manifestation of God in whom "we live and move and have our being" (Acts 17:28).

How to describe this God? There are many ways, and they open out into the images of the afterlife found in the following chapters. We can speak of the world as God's Body. As God's Body, the universe makes visible the invisible God. If God dwells in matter, it is not only good, but also sacred. The natural world is a temple of the Holy. This underscores what we know and believe, that our bodies and the bodies of all those we love are more than they might seem. So are the bodies of trees, plants, animals, and other created beings.

The Breath of God fills all creation. God as the Spirit that infuses the universe with life is as intimate and close to us as our breath. The Greek word *pneuma* translates as wind, breath, or spirit. Air carries sound, voices, and melodies to us. The rain rides on it to our windows and streams. It sustains and enlivens us. Air is the breath of life, a symbol of a more mysterious reality. The poet Denise Levertov names this mystery "God the air enveloping the whole globe of being."

Water is another ancient image of the divine. The psalmist craves God like a thirsty deer, or parched land. The divine is like a river running through all things, the wellspring from which all life flows. God is the name we give to the ground and depth of an interconnected whole. This divine spring already manifests itself in the universe, but it will well up and flow through all of creation more freely in the future. We hope one day to drink more fully from it.

If the universe is a web of beings, God is the Love that binds each element to every other. Divine Love courses through it. We hope to meet this Love face-to-face someday, as promised. If the universe is a tapestry of intricate color and design, God is the Light that illumines it from within, the Tender Care that makes each element what it is. Denise Levertov captures this ongoing mystery of creation in her poem "Primary Wonder."

> And then
> once more the quiet mystery
> is present to me, the throng's clamor
> recedes: the mystery
> that there is anything, anything at all,
> let alone cosmos, joy, memory, everything,
> rather than void: and that, O Lord,
> Creator, Hallowed One, You still,
> hour by hour sustain it

Thomas Merton calls this Mystery, within which we are all held, the Mercy of God. Each time we go to our deepest center, it opens out into the wide Mercy in all of creation. The promise that in the end God will be all in all foreshadows the fusion of immanence and transcendence, the unveiling of Mercy.

FOR PRAYER AND REFLECTION

Psalm 16

> Unnamable God, I feel you
> with me at every moment.
> You are my food, my drink,
> my sunlight, and the air I breathe.
> You are the ground I have built on
> and the beauty that rejoices my heart.
> I give thanks to you at all times
> for lifting me from my confusion,
> for teaching me in the dark
> and showing me the path of life.

I have come to the center of the universe;
I rest in your perfect love.
In your presence there is fullness of joy
and blessedness forever and ever.

—Translated by Stephen Mitchell

Remembering Our Breath

By awareness of our breathing we come to the present and to the presence of God. Breathing is a way of resting in the Spirit and of making our breath one with the Divine Breath that sustains the universe. It is also a bodily form of prayer that links us with the universe.

Breathe in the Spirit of God. Let it permeate your being, moving to every cell in your body, reviving the flame of life in you.

Breathe in the Spirit of God. Let Her hold you in love and care so that you can do that for others. Let Her love comfort and support you so that you can be there for others.

Breathe in the Spirit of God. Let it fill you with gratitude. Let it flow out to all your sisters and brothers on the planet.

—Kathleen Fischer

2. Soul Talk

Remember thou art dust,
and unto dust thou shalt return.
—Ash Wednesday Liturgy

My mother asked that her ashes be scattered in the Pacific Ocean she so loved. During one of her last visits to Cannon Beach on the Oregon coast, she pronounced it to be as close to heaven as she could get. So after her memorial service my husband and I joined several other family members there. It was nearing sunset on a windy April evening as we chose a rocky point remote from the more heavily populated areas of the beach. There we released her ashes into the wind and surf, along with rose petals and her favorite flower, long-stemmed pink carnations. My brother later wrote about the experience.

Goodbye, Eva
And God bless you

Carnations on the sand
Ashes in the wind
Ashes in the tide

Portents:
rainbows
sea gulls sweeping low
and sheet lightning

Souls swirling
Death chill

Sisters standing in the surf
paying homage in grave winds
a morbid rushing sea

Beyond grief
Small prayers and goodbyes

Scattering my mother's ashes raised viscerally for me the question, Can this be all that is left of the courageous woman who raised eight children, fed us homemade chili and fried bologna, sewed prom dresses, loved flowers and family gatherings, and endured so much mental and physical suffering for eighty-nine years? The refrain from Ash Wednesday, familiar to me since childhood, served as a somber reminder of mortality, providing no assurances.

So I returned to ancient questions about the survival of body and soul. These were no longer the theoretical matters I once debated in graduate school classes. Now they were about my own mother. My search took me from old definitions to new answers.

Body and Soul

Although there is a lot of talk about soul these days, it is seldom clear exactly what is meant. Soul can refer to many things. It may mean the life principle that accounts for a person's characteristic attributes. Or it might indicate the spiritual part of us that is distinct from the physical. When we think of a soul friend, it is someone who meets us where we are most deeply ourselves.

For many people, belief in life after death rests on the conviction that there is an immaterial part of us, the soul, that is eternal and lives on after the body dies. Plato, the Greek philosopher who lived in the fourth and fifth centuries BCE, described the human person as an immortal soul imprisoned in a mortal body. His body/soul dualism has strongly influenced Western thinking. According to such dualism, the body is the perishable part of us. At death, the soul, like a freed prisoner, flies to its eternal home in heaven. To depict this flight to freedom, the ancient Egyptians pictured the soul as a bird with a human face. Even some Christians who profess belief in the resurrection of the body speak of an actual death in these terms.

While this understanding of body and soul gives us helpful images of the death of a loved one, it is also problematic. In this world, who we are and what we love is intertwined with the material—our own bodies, those of persons we love, the Earth itself. We care too much for the material world to regard it as of only passing value. Further, contemporary science undermines this talk of soul by declaring that the human person is not two parts, the nonmaterial and the material, but only one substance, a physical body.

In response to these concerns, there are many creative efforts to find other ways of talking about body and soul and personal survival after death. My return to the topic drew me straight into this lively discussion. It is still a wide-open quest for understanding, but I find one approach most promising.

The Patterns of Creation

In his small classic, *The Lives of a Cell,* biologist Lewis Thomas says that there is a continual music in creation. He calls our attention to the percussive sounds termites make as they beat their heads against the dark resonating corridors of their nests. Or the way gorillas beat their chests for certain kinds of dialogue. Then there are the songs that toads sing, and their friends sing back in antiphony. Thomas thinks that if we had better hearing, we would detect other melodies: the descants of sea birds, the rhythmic tympani of schools of mollusks, and the harmonics of midges in sunny meadows.

There should be some explanation for this urge to make music that is so fundamental to our biology. Thomas suggests that these rhythmic sounds are the score for a transformation taking place all around us, the movement of random and chaotic matter into the improbable and ordered dance of living forms. If there were sounds to represent this process of the ever more complex organization of matter from atoms to molecules and beyond, it would for Thomas have the beauty of Bach's *Brandenburg Concertos*. But he wonders whether this process is not recapitulated by the music that surrounds us in birdsongs, whale descants, locust vibrations, and gorilla tympani.

In the universe of chaos and order that Thomas describes, it is not possible to divide beings neatly into two parts such as body and soul. What we call matter and spirit are rather two interwoven dimensions of reality. Quantum physics tells us that matter has much less substance than we thought. It is subtle, complex, and filled with possibilities for combination. In fact, matter is a form of energy. And matter/energy can act in ways that seem quite miraculous. It can become self-organizing; it can spontaneously develop patterns and structures. It makes music. Yes, we are dust. But this dust is filled with potential. The volatile death spasms of the stars were the furnace that forged elements necessary for life itself. We arose from these ashes of stellar death. We can no longer think of matter as a lifeless lump waiting to be molded like a handful of clay.

How can we talk of soul in such a universe? The mathematical physicist and Anglican priest John Polkinghorne suggests one way. He describes the soul not as something separate from the body, but as a very complex pattern or configuration that carries the information making the body uniquely itself. These patterns are intertwined with the matter/energy in the universe, but they name our intuition that there is more to nature than simple combinations of matter or transformations of energy. Something gives things a pattern or order.

We can go all the way back to the Greek philosopher Aristotle and call the soul the form of the body, as long as we keep in mind that we are using the term in a fresh way. Within a new understanding of the universe, form or organization makes life possible; it gives every existing thing identity, an integrity and peculiarity that distinguishes it from everything else. Though embedded in matter/energy, this information transcends the material in which it is embodied. All of nature is communicating in complicated ways, making music as it converts chaos into ordered patterns.

The pattern called soul arises from my genetic makeup, my past, my relationships, and my awareness and experiences. It is my full, integral identity. It grows and changes throughout my lifetime; there is an abiding whole even though individual elements are lost. For example, we remain somehow the same in spite of a constant interchange of all the atoms and molecules that make up our bodies. It does not matter that we lose thousands of cells every day. On the entry wall in our home we have a picture of my husband, Tom, when he was four. He is wearing a favorite blue-and-white sailor suit and smiling mischievously. There, in a distant moment preserved, is the same impish grin that still pops up on occasion nearly sixty years later.

In fact, I am aware that I am many selves, created from moment to moment. Each of us weaves together an enduring personal identity across time; the person we were yesterday is now a part of our being. The truth of this struck me as I read the memorial tribute for a nun who died at the age of ninety-nine. It included these words from a superior's letter to her: "There are so many things for which my head and my heart say 'Thank you' to you that I can't even list them. But I believe most of all I am thankful to God that always, throughout the long years, I find you *always you*."

Think of the way we recognize a person after years without contact. Shortly after finishing my doctoral studies, I returned to a parish in Mount Angel, Oregon, to give a talk. Mount Angel is

16

a small town a short drive from Salem, where I was born and grew up. The audience for my talk was a group of seasoned adults from the farm communities surrounding the church. I did my best to sound like a big-city scholar. During my talk, I noticed one woman studying me very closely. At the end, she came up to me and said, "Say, aren't you the little Fischer girl?"

But does this soul, this pattern or configuration that is *me*, survive the final change that is death? In our spontaneous language about those who have died, we instinctively speak of the preservation of what most characterized them, the persistence of their identity. Recently, when a senior safety with the University of Washington football team died of spinal cord injuries, his brother said of him: "He's somewhere right now and he's running fast." We believe that the unique music that is a life, the original story woven from so many strands, will continue in some way.

Who preserves these rich patterns, these tight soul/body unities of all living beings, as they pass through death? Christian teaching does not rely on the immortality of the soul, but on the transformation of the whole person. Death is real. But we believe that God will not forget us; everlastingly God remembers us. While developing a new way to speak of soul, Polkinghorne insists it is reasonable to hope that the pattern that is me will be remembered by God and re-created in a new environment of God's making. Because God will not abandon the universe, the matter of the world to come will be the transformed matter of this world. This is the full realization of the age-old language of prophetic hope.

> O dwellers in the dust, awake
> and sing for joy!
> For your dew is a radiant dew,
> and the earth will give birth to
> those long dead. (Isa 26:19)

This is also the message of Jesus' empty tomb. The resurrection of the body is not the resuscitation of our present structure. It is liberation from that decay, into a new kind of personhood.

A Hidden God

There is a Jewish tale found in Hasidic mysticism in which a rabbi's young grandson is playing hide-and-seek with some other children. Suddenly the boy comes crying to his grandfather, "I hid myself so well, and no one was looking for me." The rabbi is moved and says, "Now I know what God has been trying to tell me: 'I've hidden myself so well that no one is looking for me.'"

New ways of talking about the soul, because they assume a self-organizing universe, seem to hide the presence of God. In fact, many no longer look for God; for them, Creation is fully explained in scientific terms. But for those who believe that we are created in the image of God, the question arises, Where is God in the complex, chaotic, but ordered universe science describes?

In the current universe story, the divine influence is hidden and indirect, respectful of the open-ended freedom and creativity of all beings. God is the Mystery deep within the evolving cosmos, a Creation of amazing order and novelty, unity and diversity. The divine work is seen in the universe's passion and beauty, in the general organizing principles that hold everything together and are not reducible to the laws of physics. The philosopher Alfred North Whitehead calls God the Poet of the World, a gentle and persuasive power calling everything forward by a vision of what it might become.

This is not the God many of us were taught to believe in, the God who created the universe in a distant beginning and has since intervened on certain special occasions, like the call of Abraham or the exodus from Egypt. That God is a supernatural being who is outside and above the world, ruling it with power and might. At death we go to be with this God, if our lives pass the test of a final judgment. Much of what we do in this life is for the sake of earning heaven's rewards and avoiding hell's punishments.

But it is increasingly difficult for many to believe in this God who is King, Lawmaker, and Judge. Nor is this the only God found in the biblical and religious traditions. There are many names for God, and their abundance keeps us from making an idol out of any single image of the Holy. As we saw in the previous chapter, God is also the gracious Mystery that permeates all life and yet transcends it.

The biblical books of Wisdom and Proverbs portray God as ordering the world in the subtle and indirect way of the contemporary cosmic account. These books speak of the unseen mystery of God in the female symbol of Wisdom, who in Greek is called Sophia. One of the characteristics of Holy Wisdom, or Sophia, is her presence in all things. This is a hidden presence that has to be discovered; Wisdom is active in the coming into being of all Creation.

> She reaches mightily from one end
> of the earth to the other,
> And she orders all things well. (Wis 8:1)

Wisdom pervades the world, luring it to fuller life. In fact, she can say, "Whoever finds me, finds life" (Prov 8:35). Calling into being the things of the world, she is there when the heavens are fixed firm, the skies and foundations of the Earth established, the boundaries set to the sea. These realities are related aspects of a completed whole, but they bear significant difference. She is the source of these distinct identities.

Wisdom, human beings, and all creatures are interrelated in complex ways in sustaining Creation in its becoming. All beings contribute to God's Creation of the world as they order and pattern their experience, as they add their distinct melodies to a grand symphony. Creation is not a onetime, past event; it is ongoing, a participation in Divine Wisdom.

> Although she is but one, she can
> do all things,
> and while remaining in herself, she
> renews all things;

in every generation she passes into
holy souls
and makes them friends of God
and prophets. (Wis 7:27)

Wisdom is the source of all the patterns or souls of the universe and their relationship to one another. And she is also able to order them into a comprehensive whole.

In the Book of Wisdom, God is portrayed as delighting in the physical world for its own sake, suggesting that we are here to share the divine joy in all that is. In death we entrust ourselves and those we love to this Holy Wisdom, counting on her to continue to create ever-new forms of beauty and wholeness from our lives.

FOR PRAYER AND REFLECTION

Divine Poet of the Universe,
We sing in praise of your Presence. You are
inside us, between us, and around us, even when
we cannot sense that you are here.

Thank you for entrusting us with freedom, for
making us co-creators with you. There is joy
in this adventure of giving shape to life.

But there are also risks. We teeter at the edge of chaos,
and are afraid. We lose our way. Forces of destruction
threaten our fragile future. It is hard to fashion ourselves
into a symphony all can enjoy.

You call us to a greatness we can hardly envision.
Open us more fully to your vision of truth, beauty, goodness, and love. Help us imagine possibilities of peace in
the heart of hatred, of nonviolence in the midst of
violence.

In the darkest of nights, may we attend to those persons
who embody your dream and so light our way. Teach us
that we all shape the future. Though our imprints remain
hidden, nothing we do is insignificant.

And when our lives begin to shatter
like shards of broken glass,
when the final darkness that is death arrives,
remember, Creator of the Universe, that we are yours.

—Kathleen Fischer

A Meditation on Sophia

Meditation lets the words of a passage gradually deepen
within us.

Begin with some quiet breathing and centering of your mind
and body. Then repeat silently these descriptions of biblical
Wisdom, God's presence in the world, allowing them to rest in
your heart and mind. Let the images they evoke arise in you.

If you are drawn to a particular word or phrase, stay with it for
a time. Pray whatever it is that stirs in you.

She gave to holy people the
reward of their labors;
she guided them along a
marvelous way,
and became a shelter to them by
day,
and a starry flame through the
night. (Wis 10:17)

She is more beautiful than the sun
and excels every constellation of
the stars.

Compared with the light she is
found to be superior,
for it is succeeded by the night,
but against wisdom evil does not
prevail. (Wis 7:29–30)

My fruit is better than gold, even
fine gold,
and my yield than choice silver.
I walk in the way of
righteousness,
along the paths of justice,
endowing with wealth those who
love me,
and filling their treasuries. (Prov 8:19–21)

When you are finished meditating on the passages, remain
a few moments in silence, or close with a favorite prayer.

—Kathleen Fischer

3. Metamorphosis

One fine spring morning she pierces the shroud
and comes out a butterfly. That is how in us,
through the darkness, deliverance is busy.
                                    —Nikos Kazantzakis

lisabeth Kübler-Ross, the Swiss psychiatrist who got us talking about death, was a relief worker in the Maidanek concentration camp during World War II. She found the stench, the barbed wire, the smoking chimneys, and the boxes of baby shoes wrenching. But what moved her most was the scribbling on the walls of the empty barracks. There, in the midst of graffiti and hundreds of initials carved into the five-tiered wooden bunks, were countless drawings of butterflies. Days or hours before dying in the gas chambers, children and adults left this final message: the butterfly, symbol of transformation.

The career of the caterpillar illustrates the marvel of metamorphosis. A living thing of a certain kind can be transformed into a living thing of a different kind. Well, what about me? When I die, might I also change into a reality wonderfully new and beautiful? Is there a butterfly-like continuity in discontinuity that preserves the identity of all living beings even as death comes upon them?

Though the butterfly may seem too flimsy a metaphor for so weighty a subject, it has long been considered an apt image for life after death. The butterfly's tale of transformation goes like this: A wormlike larva spins a silky envelope and then is remade. By the time its chrysalis breaks, the caterpillar has changed from a crawling, woolly creature to a slender, winged flash of color. Its hue, shape, and mode of moving about are all dramatically different. It emerges gloriously new, bearing only traces of its origin in the caterpillar once confined to a cocoon. Its metamorphosis is as much a marvel as a donkey becoming a bird, or a bear becoming an eagle.

Nature as Parable

The butterfly is not an anomaly. Metamorphosis happens throughout nature in ways large and small. This offers us hope— to be sure, fragile and precarious—that life can spring from death. I pondered this some years ago when a volcano flattened the peak of Washington State's Mount St. Helens, tossed trees like matchsticks onto nearby hillsides, and covered adjacent meadows with a pallid gray blanket. That was May 18, 1980. All seemed lost. One month later, ferns and lilies had begun to push their green shoots up through the ash. Tiny mammals emerged from their burrows and resumed their multiplication. On every visit since then, I find the revival continuing.

I encountered another example of metamorphosis in the petrified forest of northeastern Arizona. There, wood that has turned to stone lies scattered across the desert. Living trees have become semiprecious stones. How did this happen? Wood from primitive trees tumbled downstream and was buried by mud and sand. But this ancient mud contained ash from neighboring volcanoes. Released into the water, the ash seeped into the logs. Gradually crystals formed and grew, turning the trees to stone. More mud and sand from the streams buried the logs, protecting them from decay. This petrified wood is harder than steel, yet brittle as glass. In millions of further years, erosion may change it again to grains of sand.

Transfiguration occurs on an even larger scale in the universe itself. A sequence of changes connects the atoms of our bodies to the whole cosmos. The early universe transformed itself many times, with matter taking on ever new forms. The old gives rise to the new: hydrogen nuclei, protons, galaxies, stars, condensed dust particles, planets. We observe the same phenomenon when we trace the history of life on Earth. There is increasing complexity from the first biomolecules to the vast panoply of microbes, fungi, plants, animals, and human beings. Each stage carries the old within it, but in a qualitatively new form. On every level, nature provides a parable of shifting shapes.

Resurrection as Transformation

The metamorphosis found in nature is perhaps easier to acknowledge than the transformation described in the stories of Jesus' resurrection. The idea of bodily resurrection is a stumbling block for many today. But transformation is also the hinge on which the meaning of resurrection turns. When the risen Jesus appears to his disciples, they have trouble recognizing him. He is the same Jesus with whom they walked and shared meals, but now somehow so different that they do not know him. Jesus' appearances are like finding an old friend so changed after many years that we walk right past her and do a doubletake when we slowly realize who she is. In each Easter story there are just such moments of not knowing and then suddenly recognizing Jesus.

Consider, for example, Jesus' appearance to Mary Magdalene as told near the end of John's Gospel. It is just before dawn. Mary peers into Jesus' tomb and finds it empty. She is distraught as she takes the measure of her loss. When Jesus himself stands before her, she does not know him and mistakes him for the gardener. She answers his question, "Whom do you seek?" with a tearful reporting of Jesus' missing body and laments that someone must have taken him away.

Preoccupied as she is with the physical absence of Jesus, Mary is not prepared for his new presence. Jesus says to her, "Mary!" Now called by name herself, she realizes who he is. Our natural impulse at such a moment would be to embrace and hold fast this person we feared we had lost forever. But Jesus tells Mary,

"Do not continue to touch me," but go tell the others what you have experienced. In other words, Mary is not to try to relate to Jesus as if things were *status quo*; he has not simply been resuscitated from the dead. He is different now. He is in glory, that is, in the fullness of God's presence. Mary is to return to the community, which is where she will now find the presence of Jesus in the world.

The other accounts of Jesus' resurrection appearances contain this same theme. Jesus walks alongside a couple of his disciples on their way to Emmaus.

> While they were talking and discussing, Jesus himself came near and went with them, but their eyes were kept from recognizing him. (Luke 24:15–16)

Jesus and the two travelers have a long talk and share a meal, and it is only then, as they eat together, that they realize who Jesus is. The next thing they know, he has vanished.

To Change and Yet Remain the Same

The first witnesses to the resurrection do not try to explain in any simple way their experience of Jesus as the same yet different. Nor do they clean up the contradictions in their stories. The doubt, fear, and derision are left in the account for readers to see. They do not hide the fact that some are frightened, thinking they have seen a ghost. Still, they become convinced that this is the pre-Easter Jesus in a different mode of presence. They have met the familiar in an unfamiliar embodiment. Jesus' body is wonderfully new, but it bears vestiges of all that has gone before.

Debate has raged for centuries on whether the resurrection was an objective event or simply a changed consciousness among Jesus' followers. There are no signs that agreement will soon be reached. Furthermore, this way of posing the question seems increasingly futile, something like asking whether science or poetry is the real way to truth.

Like all complex human events, the appearances of the risen Jesus happen on both the inside and the outside. Details like Jesus' eating of fish or inviting Thomas to touch his wounds suggest an objective event. But change clearly happens inside the witnesses as well. Their hearts are burning within them. They are convinced this is the same Jesus they knew. Empirical details are provided, but the experience is more than these facts. A deeper kind of recognition is taking place.

The fact that it is women who first see the risen Christ may help clarify this kind of knowing. Full recognition in the Easter stories may require the relational knowing more characteristic of women, which is marked by bodily memory, intuition, and emotional understanding. Jesus appears to those with whom he has a personal relationship. They recognize him as participants, not as detached bystanders; they are known and called by name. To sense the difference between these two kinds of knowledge, think of the contrast between the curious onlookers and the friends and family of survivors who are being welcomed back from a mining accident or a military battle.

The resurrection appearances are *stories*. Perhaps story is the only way metamorphosis can be portrayed, the only way we can talk about Jesus' resurrection and our own. As historian Carolyn Walker-Bynum puts it: "Story has before and after, gain and loss." The change, the miracle, the surprise, are spread over time. Transformation becomes apparent only as we watch the self take new forms, each replacing the one before it. All our lives we are changing, aging, dying, and yet remaining recognizably the same. Like a butterfly we carry our selves lightly amid metamorphosis.

This is what Paul is talking about as he tries to describe our resurrection from death to the Corinthians.

So it is with the resurrection of the dead. What is sown is perishable, what is raised is imperishable. It is sown in dishonor, it is raised in glory. It is sown in weakness, it is raised in power. It is sown a physical body, it is raised a spiritual body. (1 Cor 15:42–44)

FOR PRAYER AND REFLECTION

Easter Greetings

We greet you with the growing warmth of springtime
and the promise of summer.
We greet you with the flowers that open their buds to the
sun and the green grass that shoots out of the earth.
We greet you with peoples scourged by war and poverty,
peoples seeking to let the transforming presence
enable them to pass on hope to their children.
We greet you with those who suffer physical, emotional, or
moral sickness or pain.
We greet you with all our preoccupations with the past or
the future, our concerns about security and how we
look, our difficulties accepting the present moment of grace.
We greet you with the amazing variety of peoples.
We greet you with all our differences in hearing each
other, of forgiving one another, of letting go of old hurts.
We greet you with the Spirit of Love that freely moves in
each of our cells and throughout our veins and deep in
the marrow of our bones.
The great stones roll away.

—Phil Prudhomme and Kitty Custer

Living God,
Let me learn the lesson of the butterfly:

to trust the marvel of metamorphosis,
to believe when there is only darkness,

28

to hang tough in times of change,
to fear less the new and different,
to release my grip and let go.

Thank you for putting all around us parables of
our final morphing into something wondrously new.

—Kathleen Fischer

4. Amazing Seeds

The Moon of Ripening Berries waned,
and its fruits fell to the ground or hung on
stems like drops of blood. Death seemed
to be everywhere. Yet in the fruit
were seeds.

       — Bunny McBride

he seed is an ancient metaphor for life after death. It carries all the elements of hope: decay and death, darkness, endurance, emergence of life in forms impossible to predict. There is cause for amazement when a bundle of tiny seeds explodes into a field of multicolored wildflowers, when a nut small enough to fit in the hollow of a hand soars into a giant oak tree.

Attempts to imagine how it is possible to survive death frequently rely on the discussion of seeds found in 1 Corinthians 15. This is Paul's chosen metaphor for answering questions posed by Christians in the vibrant Greek city of Corinth. It is about 56 CE, not long after Jesus' crucifixion and resurrection appearances, but the Corinthians' questions are contemporary: How can a body decay in the ground and yet rise again? What sort of body could that possibly be?

A Different Kind of Bodily Existence

A grain dies, and finds life again in a different body. And there is continuity between the seed and the plant. Paul suggests that something like this happens in resurrection. His comparison is perhaps easier to grasp while driving past fields of wheat, golden and glorious in the late afternoon sunlight. The swaying stalks do not resemble rotting seed, but that is what they sprang from.

By means of his seed analogy, Paul makes several crucial points. In resurrection, an open-ended transformation is happening. The sprouting wheat indeed differs from the bare seed. But it is not entirely different. The grain is not the same form, or perhaps even made of the same stuff, as the seed, but something accounts for identity.

In trying to convey both this change and the ongoing connection, Paul calls the resurrected body a *spiritual* body, but it has always been hard to figure out exactly what he means. One clue is that the *spiritual* person Paul talks about in the rest of his letter to the Corinthians is not some sort of ethereal reality, but an ordinary person who has been made new by the Spirit of God. Paul is not thinking of a disembodied soul that escapes death. For him, the human person is a unity. The *whole* person moves into a new Spirit-filled existence, and then is changed again in death. Like us, Paul is groping for redemption language that entails not just body, and not just spirit, but both.

Further, he wants to make clear that the resurrected body is not simply a resuscitated dead body, a grand version of the medical rescue efforts occurring in modern cities. Death is real, and the contrast between this present body and what Paul calls the spiritual body is as great as that between a decaying seed and a sheaf of wheat. Theologians speak of continuity within discontinuity to describe this identity and difference between dying and risen bodies.

The Spiritual Body as Social Body

By using the term *spiritual body*, Paul is probably also trying to convey a sense of the body as connectedness rather than separation. He would be drawing here on the Hebraic understanding of the body as source of solidarity. It is hard to imagine this different kind

31

of bodily existence when we are so conditioned to viewing ourselves as separate individuals narrowly confined within our bodies. But the body is in fact what joins every individual with every other, and with the entire cosmos. Our bodies link us globally with all living things, backward to the first stardust, seas, and prehistoric creatures, and outward to the peoples of the globe and the galaxies.

In the English language, *identity* is a term we use for a singular subject. However, this preoccupation with the individual is not what characterizes the resurrection appearance stories. The risen Jesus moves into a new relationship with the entire cosmos. No longer restricted by ordinary limitations of space and time, he is present to all times and places. This suggests that bodily resurrection is not simply a ticket to private salvation. It is the healing of relationships between human beings and nature, between individuals and communities, and between generation and generation. In other words, bodily transformation is not primarily about the condition of my individual body. It is hope for a transfiguration of the relational web that constitutes each of us, for a new shape to the company we keep.

The contemporary novelist Alice Sebold captures something of what this healing might look like. In her book *The Lovely Bones*, she tells the story of Susie Salmon, a fourteen-year-old girl who is raped and murdered. From the spirit world, Susie intently watches her family and friends, narrating for us the slow and painful steps they take through grief and subsequent mending. Toward the end of the story Susie says:

These were the lovely bones that had grown around my absence: the connections—sometimes tenuous, sometimes made at great cost, but often magnificent—that happened after I was gone. And I began to see things in a way that let me hold the world without me in it. The events that my death wrought were merely the bones of a body that would become whole at some unpredictable time in the future. The price of what I came to see as this miraculous body had been my life.

The worst kind of nightmare a family can face, the tragic loss of a child, is gradually transformed into new connections, new bones of love and hope among those left behind.

Centuries earlier, Paul used not only the language of *body*, but also the metaphor of *temple* to talk about the making whole of lives torn apart by suffering and tragedy. In fact, he talks of the body *as* temple. It is another way of saying that belief in resurrection drastically changes our thinking about God, bodies, and relationships.

According to Paul, Jesus' resurrection means that all of us together constitute the sanctuary where God dwells with women and men now and forever.

> Do you not know that you [plural] are God's temple and that God's Spirit dwells in you?...For God's temple is holy, and you [plural] are that temple. (1 Cor 3:16–17)

We think of a temple as simply a designated place of worship, a building of immovable stones. One can venture inside and perhaps have an experience of God. But here is the surprising resurrection message: We are God's building. You and I and all of us together are living stones, each distinct, but together comprising the temple where God dwells. The temple is not just a cold brick structure. Its building blocks encompass the drug addict serving a prison term, the aging couple who ride our bus, the nineteen-year-old Chinese woman who dies of exhaustion from working in a stuffed-toy factory, the homeless woman who each night pushes her grocery cart of belongings to another storefront.

The Gospels make this same link between the life to come and the present life. Love and resurrection belong together not only because we long to meet again those we love who have died. Our hope is for more, not less, than that. It looks to the restoration of the world itself. This is part of the point of the familiar last judgment scene in Matthew's Gospel, where we are told that when we gave food to the hungry, drink to the thirsty, and clothes to the naked, we met God. What you and I do now with one another has lasting significance.

A Jewish rabbinic story expresses this truth. It can serve as a parable of amazing seeds and paradise.

Time before time, when the world was young, two brothers shared a field and a mill, each night dividing evenly the grain they had ground together during the day. One brother lived alone; the other had a wife and a large family. Now the single brother thought to himself one day, "It isn't really fair that we divide the grain evenly. I have only myself to care for, but my brother has children to feed." So each night he secretly took some of his grain to his brother's granary to see that he was never without.

But the married brother said to himself one day, "It isn't really fair that we divide the grain evenly, because I have children to provide for me in my old age, but my brother has no one. What will he do when he's old?" So every night he secretly took some of *his* grain to his brother's granary. As a result, both of them always found their supply of grain mysteriously replenished each morning.

Then one night they met each other halfway between their two houses, suddenly realized what had been happening, and embraced each other in love. The story is that God witnessed their meeting and proclaimed, "This is a holy place—a place of love—and here it is that my temple shall be built." And so it was.

The prophets and early Christians all looked forward to a new age that would be ushered in by the coming of God's Glory, a time when the divine presence would fill the Earth. The startling message of Jesus' resurrection is that the end time has already begun.

Living On in Glory

In the Bible, our destiny and that of all creation is called glory: "I consider that the sufferings of this present time are not worth comparing with the glory about to be revealed to us" (Rom 8:18). Hymns and prayers also refer to heaven as glory. But such references to glory seem insubstantial, like the clouds that frequently drift into depictions of heaven. What do they mean?

Glory, like clouds, is a symbol of presence. In the Hebrew Bible, the glory of God signifies the visible, movable divine presence. The prophets hope that it will fill the Earth. In Jewish writings after the close of the biblical canon, the Spirit of God is called the *shekinah,* from the Hebrew word that means "to dwell." *Shekinah* becomes a synonym for God's presence. She appears in the symbols of cloud, fire, and light—but especially in divine glory. *Shekinah,* or the divine radiance, unexpectedly shines forth in places where the world is especially bent and broken. So when we read that Jesus entered into glory, and we will as well, it means coming into the fullness of the divine presence. The Eastern church describes our future as deification, human nature filled with the divine, the way it was meant to be.

Through all the discussions of resurrection, belief that life after death is somehow *bodily* has endured. Something very fundamental to hope is at stake in the paradox of the abstract terms *continuity* and *discontinuity.* It is this: God does not throw away the first creation, scrap it as it were, and start fresh. Like an artist who reshapes clay rather than tossing it away, God uses the old as the basis of the new. This anchors the everlasting value of physical existence, even amid bodily frailty and deterioration.

The seed analogy situates hope precisely where hurt and horror occur, in the shutting down of the bodily systems that sustain us. While death can be peaceful and quiet, it can also be wrenching and ugly. Today's news carries the account of a sixty-three-year-old mother who walked into the nursing home where her two sons, both in their early forties, lay side by side. Each was in the advanced stages of the Huntington's disease that had slowly killed their father and now rendered them inarticulate. The mother shot them to death and then calmly waited in the lobby to be arrested. Though we cannot imagine how it is possible to find redemption in a scene of such physical carnage, belief in bodily resurrection says that glory will somehow touch down right here.

Belief in bodily resurrection anchors our care for the entire creation. How could the resurrection of Jesus be a denial of the physical universe? He valued it so much that he made it the basis of his parables, those stories about what it is like to know the presence of God. The here and now is what will be made into glory: the world of children who throw tantrums and neighbors who let their dogs run loose, of volunteers who save forests and politicians who sell wetlands, of wedding celebrations and family quarrels. John, the poet and seer who penned the fourth Gospel, speaks mainly about *life* in his narrative. We enjoy even now a divine reality that is powerful enough to survive death, just as it gave Jesus victory over death: "I am the resurrection and the life. Those who believe in me, even though they die, will live, and everyone who lives and believes in me will never die" (John 11:25–26).

Jesus' resurrection shows that it is possible for a human being to bear evil and emerge from evil. The unhealed and the downright ugly in the universe, the pain of poverty and injustice, the desperate struggle to beat back decay and failure, the despair before endless war and violence and fleeing refugees—this is what is redeemed. Right in the midst of the unspeakably worst and most painful of human experiences, there is promise of glory. The seed that is planted and dies, not something else entirely, emerges as the marvelous plant.

FOR PRAYER AND REFLECTION

When the signs of age begin to mark my body (and still more when they touch my mind); when the ill that is to diminish me or carry me off strikes from without or is born within me; when the painful moment comes in which I suddenly awaken to the fact that I am ill or growing old; and above all at that last moment when I feel I am losing hold of myself and am absolutely passive within the hands of the great unknown forces that have formed me; in all those dark moments, O God, grant that I may understand that it is you (provided only my faith is strong enough) who are painfully parting the fibres of my being in order to penetrate to the very marrow of my substance and bear me away within yourself.

—Teilhard de Chardin

Spirit of God,
Bless this universe of yearning, our living, dying world.
Make fertile our soil for your seeds of love.
Teach us to honor our bodies and your Body, the Earth.
Fill us afresh with hope of redemption.
Surrounded by darkness, we long for your glory.

—Kathleen Fischer

5. Awareness

The foetus,
expert at attachment,
didn't dream that
cramped canal would open
into sound and light and love—
it clung. It didn't care. The future
looked like death to it, from there.
— Heather McHugh

From ancient to modern times, a common thread runs through the literature of hope: the incompleteness of what we now know when compared with what is to come. Examples large and small of our limited perception abound. There are colors we cannot see, and sounds we do not hear, because we are simply not equipped to do so. Even physicists are unable to picture all the dimensions of space. Depictions of the afterlife anticipate the fulfillment not only of heart, but of mind as well. We will be fully aware.

A friend whose daily meditation practice comes from the Buddhist tradition talks about her conviction that death will lead to greater awareness. This belief does not take away her sense of separation and grief when someone close dies, she says, or her shrinking from the pain and diminishment of the dying process: "It does take away my fear though, because I think we experience such a tiny iota of life now and I believe I will experience more awareness of all aspects of *LIFE* after death. I cannot say I know this intellectually, but I sense it profoundly." The veil will lift at death, revealing what has been hidden.

This belief raises questions about how awareness survives death, bringing us into dialogue with contemporary studies of the mind. Those investigations are themselves knotted with quandaries. The neuroscientist Antonio Damasio uses the metaphor of stepping into the light for the birth of human consciousness. Understanding just how we are aware of our own selves and our environs is the leading frontier in the life sciences, the final mystery that seems insoluble. Is it possible to comprehend how we know suffering and pleasure, shame and pride? Can we possibly fathom how we are able to create art, science, technology, and social and political organizations? Even when we have made a dent in understanding these aspects of the workings of mind, Damasio says, there will still be enough mystery left to last many scientific lifetimes, and enough wonder to keep us modest for some time to come.

One aspect of this mystery is how awareness can exist without the physical brain. There are those who say it cannot, because science will soon be able to explain the mind in completely physical terms. If everything in nature can be reduced to its most fundamental aspects, then when the brain dies, so does consciousness. But this is only one among many positions in a lively debate.

This dialogue addresses many critical questions: Will the individual self-awareness we prize so much survive death? Will it change into another state of consciousness or merge into a wider reality? Can we lose our personal names and still know joy? Does it matter? Answers to such questions take different turns.

The Brain As a Window to God

While visiting India some years ago, my husband and I often passed saffron-robed monks sitting motionless in meditation. So altered was their state of consciousness that they took no notice of the flies buzzing around their heads or the noisy conversations next to them. Back home I have attended workshops in recent years on the latest brain-imaging techniques. I watched different regions of the brain light up and saw that this area is implicated in Parkinson's disease, that one in depression. I learned that certain aspects of consciousness are related to specific brain regions and systems, that there is a brain architecture that can be photographed and analyzed.

These two events may seem unrelated, but not for researchers who are bringing together brain science and the biology of belief. In *Why God Won't Go Away*, Andrew Newberg and Eugene D'Aquili report on their study of the relationship between religious experience and brain function. Using state-of-the-art brain-imaging cameras, they recorded the spiritual experiences of Tibetan Buddhist meditators and Franciscan nuns. When they looked at images of the brain states that correspond to these experiences, they were able to identify the region of the brain associated with religious experience.

In the top rear section of the brain is a small area that orients us in physical space. The technical term for this region is the *posterior superior parietal lobe*, but Newberg and D'Aquili refer to it in simpler terms as the orientation association area. This area of the brain tells us which end is up, and helps us judge angles and distances so that we can negotiate the physical landscape. To perform this function, it must generate a clear sense of the physical limits of the self. In other words, it must distinguish between the individual and everything else that makes up the universe. Because this is a demanding assignment, this brain area is ordinarily the center of furious neurological activity. But the researchers found that the scans taken at the peak of their subjects' meditative states show a sharp reduction in activity levels in this orientation area. At the deepest point of meditation, the brain is unable to find any boundaries. It perceives the self as endlessly and intimately interwoven with everyone and everything.

Newberg and D'Aquili conclude that neurology does not contradict what mystical reality holds, that there is a deeper self beneath the subjective awareness we call the self. Underlying the mind's perception of thoughts, memories, emotions, and objects, there exists a state of awareness that sees beyond the limits of subject and object, matter and mind. It rests in a universe where all things are one, in which mind and body are aspects of a larger whole.

Some researchers might say that finding the biology beneath transcendent experience means that God is not real, but rather "all in your mind." That is not how Newberg and D'Aquili see it. In this present life, they say, there is no way for God to get into our heads except through the brain's neural pathways. But they do not doubt that the transcendent states themselves are real. They suggest that the brain has developed the ability to transcend material existence, and to experience another plane of being that actually exists. Science, they say, has surprised them. Their inquiry goes against the assumption that nothing can be more real than a universe that can be weighed and measured. The results of their research leave them no choice but to conclude that the mystics are in fact experiencing the presence of a higher spiritual power. In other words, the mind provides a window through which human beings can catch a glimpse of the ultimately real, or the divine. And that transcendent reality cannot be reduced to the neural circuitry of the human brain.

Life After Death as Awakening

There are several belief systems that view death as a transition to another state of consciousness. Among these are forms of Hinduism and Buddhism. In Buddhist traditions, the mind is located in the body, but not limited to it. The consciousness that leaves the body at death rides on a very subtle physical form that is known as *rLung* in Tibetan, *prana* in Sanskrit, and *ch'i* in Chinese. These terms mean wind, air, subtle breath, or energy.

41

The Hindu scriptures compare the changing of physical bodies at death to changing worn-out clothes. Consciousness is always connected to the physical, but it is not bound by the body's physical form. Follow either the physical or the mental far enough, and it will lead you to the other. They are not two halves of a whole, lying side by side, but two dimensions of a larger whole.

Hinduism and Buddhism are each complex religious traditions with many branches. They depict in different ways the stages of consciousness a person passes through on the way to enlightenment. In a later chapter I will reflect on what this means for belief in reincarnation. What interests us here is the final stage beyond the cycle of death and rebirth. What is enlightenment or liberation?

The meaning of final liberation in Hinduism hinges on understanding two terms: Atman and Brahman. Brahman is the Ultimate Reality that grounds the entire universe. Atman is the human self, sometimes known as the soul or the real self. To be truly enlightened is to know that Brahman, the One that laid the foundations of the universe and sustains it, is the same as the deepest reality within my human soul. As the Upanishads, or Hindu scriptures, says:

> That which is the finest essence—this whole world has that as its soul. That is Reality. That is Atman. That art thou.

To increase awareness of this truth, both Hindus and Buddhists begin with attention to the breath. Breath is the connection that moves between inward and outward. It is as close to us as our very selves, yet it permeates the universe.

Although the soul and the divine have distinct names—Atman and Brahman—they cannot be said to be two. Because we do not always recognize this, our sense of self, the world, and God is illusory. An ancient story captures this for us. It is called "The Golden Eagle":

A man found an eagle's egg and put it in the nest of a back-yard hen. The eaglet hatched with the brood of chicks and grew up with them.

All his life the eagle did what the backyard chickens did, thinking he was a backyard chicken. He scratched the earth for worms and insects. He clucked and cackled. And he would thrash his wings and fly a few feet into the air like the chickens. After all, that is how a chicken is supposed to fly, isn't it?

Years passed and the eagle grew very old. One day he saw a magnificent bird far above him in the cloudless sky. It floated in graceful majesty among the powerful wind currents, with scarcely a beat of its strong golden wings.

The old eagle looked up in awe. "Who's that?" he said to his neighbor.

"That's the eagle, the king of the birds," said his neighbor. "But don't give it another thought. You and I are different from him."

So the eagle never gave it another thought. He died thinking he was a backyard chicken.

Like this eagle, we live with a constant case of mistaken identity. The prayer of the Upanishads asks for the wisdom to realize this:

From untruth, lead me to truth.
From darkness, lead me to light.
From death, lead me to immortality.
Om, peace, peace, peace.

What ferries one across the river of birth and death to the far shore is the wisdom of knowing that whether we go to the deepest inner reaches of ourselves or to the infinite beyond, the Real is One, and we are one with it.

Buddhist understanding of liberation is based on that of Hinduism, but shaped by its founder and distinct philosophy. The word *Buddha* means "one who is awake." It comes from the experience that Siddhartha Gautama, the historical Buddha, had one night while sitting in deep meditation under the Tree of Enlightenment. When he saw into the heart of reality, he woke up. He passed beyond the world of intellectual distinctions and opposites, and reached the state where reality appears as undivided oneness.

Siddhartha was searching for the cause of suffering. He identified it in the clinging that causes illusion, the attachments that blind us to the true nature of reality. To counter this, one should follow the eightfold noble path: an ethics respecting all that exists; insight into the true nature of things; and the cultivation of the mind through meditation. Once I am free from the desire for permanence and identity, I can relate truly to all things. I learn compassion.

In his novel *Siddhartha*, Herman Hesse describes what it means to learn the art of listening to reality in this way. Siddhartha has heard the river of life, with all its different voices, before, but now it sounds different.

> They all belonged to each other: the lament of those who yearn, the laughter of the wise, the cry of indignation and the groan of the dying. They were all interwoven and interlocked, entwined in a thousand ways. And all the voices, all the goals, all the yearnings, all the sorrow, all the pleasure, all the good and evil, all of them together was the world. All of them together was the stream of events, the music of life.

Siddhartha learns to listen attentively to this song of a thousand voices. When at last he hears the unity of them all, the great song consists of one word—*Om* or perfection. Buddhists call the far shore of the river of life and death enlightenment or *nirvana*. It brings freedom from the endless cycle of death and rebirth. It is the end of suffering, the highest peace, beyond words or thoughts.

Staying Awake Now

We often say that someone who has died has fallen asleep. That is what it looks like, of course. But as we have seen, many traditions see the afterlife as exactly the opposite, as awakening and awareness. Fullness of life, whether now or after death, depends on waking up.

Jesus' parables make that point. We are to have our lamps lit and ready. You can never tell when a given moment of life will open out into the divine. There is, for example, the story of the ten bridesmaids in Matthew's Gospel. All ten take their lamps to meet the bridegroom, but five have extra oil with them and five do not. The wait drags on, and they all fall asleep. It is midnight by the time the cry comes to light the lamps. By then those without an extra supply of oil have to go out and buy some, and they return to find the doors to the wedding hall closed. The lesson they learn: "Keep awake therefore, for you know neither the day nor the hour" (25:13).

Although the world's different contemplative traditions understand and name Ultimate Reality in a variety of ways, their goal is to take us to this place of being mindful and attentive. The point for our present purposes is that there we discover premonitions of *eternal life*: in moments of greater awareness, in prayer that opens us to a larger Mystery, in meditation where Atman and Brahman are experienced as One, in glimmers that all reality is a unity that includes us. When we are attentive, heaven and Earth meet.

FOR PRAYER AND REFLECTION

Haiku is a form of spiritual poetry that points to the Mystery experienced in the most ordinary aspects of life. The two following are by the American poet James Luguri.

Thin kite strings
Connect a handful of children
With the sky.
Even the most
gnarled of plumtrees never
lets a spring go by.

Centering Prayer

There are many ways to practice the attention that opens us to greater awareness. Here is one:

Sit relaxed and quiet.
Be in faith and love to the Mystery that dwells in the center of your being and the universe.
Take up a short word (like Mercy, Love, Peace) and let it be gently present, supporting your openness to that Mystery.
Whenever you become aware of anything else, gently use your word to return to the Mystery.
End your centering with a favorite prayer.

—Kathleen Fischer

Part II

Do Relationships Continue Beyond Death?

જી

6. In the Company of Friends

*My true self is found only
in communion with others.*
—Cynthia Bourgeault

scar Hijuelos's novel *Mr. Ives' Christmas* opens just as Ives learns that his seventeen-year-old son Robert is dead. It is a few days before Christmas, and Robert has been at a late-afternoon choir practice. As he lingers outside the church talking with a friend, a passing teenager guns him down.

Later that evening Ives sits in his son's room, trying to imagine death as something transcendent and beautiful, as he had once been taught and now longs to believe. Suddenly he feels a painful nostalgia for the kind of afterlife he was raised to believe in, heaven as a pastoral location in the clouds. In that setting people in white robes live in an eternal state of harmony with God and the saints. It is a place of perpetual love and comfort. Over the years Ives waits for a sign that his son is somewhere like that, somewhere safe and loved by God.

Though it is portrayed in imagery that no longer works for him, the community of love that Ives desires is a well-grounded way to picture life after death. Hopeful futures in this life, as well as the next, place us squarely in the company of others. Followers of Mahayana Buddhism believe that those who reach enlightenment, *bodhisattvas*, choose to remain in this world until all beings find this same joy. The prophet Ezekiel's familiar vision of a valley filled with dry bones is about a restored people, not a reassembled individual. Gospel stories teem with community gatherings that are no longer as flawed as the only ones we now know. There are dinners without discord, families free of cut-off, cities at peace.

A culture built on rugged individualism does not prepare us to share an afterlife with others, any more than it helps us see that our present well-being is linked with that of all beings in the universe. Communal depictions of future hope make sense only when we appreciate just how intrinsically relational life really is.

We Have No Self Cut Off from Others

In her poem "Sunrise," Mary Oliver talks of climbing familiar hills just as dawn breaks. As she ascends, she recalls those whose deaths, whether for an idea or for the world, create a blaze of light in the universe. Then she imagines China, India, and Europe, and how the sun shines joyfully for everyone just as it does for her. She thinks:

I am so many!
What is my name?

What is the name
of the deep breath I would take
over and over
for all of us?

Oliver's poem suggests how each element of the universe is continually interacting with all the rest. There is a constant exchange of energy, matter, and information. We breathe the planets. Some ten quadrillion bacteria live in my body. The inanimate calcified world supports me as my bone structure. Matter is a web of relationships. In this swirl of energy, the tiniest particles are woven into a unifying whole. What we have is a "physics of intimacy," relationships defining and influencing us from within.

Global labor practices highlight our connectedness from another angle. American companies that sell hiking shoes determine the standard of living and the health care of young workingwomen in the Philippines. Changes in French fashion have immense impact on the livelihood of sheep farmers in Australia. A Hmong proverb notes the way we are bundled together: "One stick cannot cook a meal or build a fence."

Put in terms of gene science, the snippets of DNA code that together make each person unique are scattered about in other genomes all over the universe. When information on genetic research first trickled out, it came as a surprise that only a few tweaks of the genetic strand separate a human being from a mouse or a chimpanzee. The message revealed by our genes is the unity of all living beings. We exist in a tangle of relationships, like overlapping footprints in the sand after a crowded day at the beach.

Rethinking Space and Time

Words about time and space permeate our language for the afterlife: *up*, *down*, and *everlasting*. Most arise from understanding space and time as something that separates rather than unites us. For example, the usual notion of space could be compared to living in separate cubicles. I am at this point and you are at that point in a sort of empty vacuum. Space keeps us and everything else apart. The same is true of time. If it is a straight line, then we are at different points on that line, separated from our forebears and our progeny. In this commonsense view of space and time, life feels like a stream of cars on a freeway, each with a single occupant isolated and sealed in a tin machine. Observed from an overpass or airplane, this rushing freeway traffic looks like a line of disconnected individuals, each plunging headlong toward some separate destination.

But contemporary physics calls into question this understanding of space and time as that which separates us. What we call space is really a field of greater and lesser densities of matter/energy. We need to change our image of life from one of fragmented individuals, like the cars on the freeway, to a moving stream without sharp divisions or separations. Our lives and actions flow and merge into one another. Images of a river or a dance capture the way we all overlap and are physically interwoven. All times, too, converge in us, so that each living organism is a "sheaf of time," a "bouquet of time." The past is still alive in the present. Even the future is already coming to be in the present.

When we move to a larger sense of the spatial and the temporal, we find that they are categories for describing not separation, but relationships. We do in actuality exist somewhere, but we are also potentially involved in everything else's becoming. In turn, we take in possibilities from other aspects of creation and make something new with them.

According to quantum physics, though we live in a particular place and time, we exist in relation to everything else. Even elemental matter is condensed energy waiting to combine in new and unpredictable ways. We are potentially an aspect of the becoming of every new reality. In this sense we are, in fact, omnipresent. My impact on the moon may be very small, but she does nothing without affecting me, nor I without affecting her. You might say that, even at the subatomic level, everybody is implicated in everybody else's business.

Physicist David Bohm calls this insight of twentieth-century science "undivided wholeness in flowing movement." He means that everything is interrelated in one fluid cosmos. The world is constantly coming in and flowing out. Life is less like Lego building blocks and more like a great river. Though she does not apply her insight to life after death, psychoanalyst Luce Irigaray believes that in such a universe "everywhere and always we can continue to embrace."

A Love Stronger Than Death

To realize the many implications of such interrelatedness in the face of death, we have only to think of the loss of someone we love. Part of *us* is ripped away. In *A Grief Observed*, C. S. Lewis describes the death of his wife, Joy. He compares it to the amputation of a limb.

> After the operation either the wounded stump heals or the man dies. If it heals, the fierce, continuous pain will stop. Presently he'll get back his strength and be able to stump about on his wooden leg. He has "got over it." But he will probably have recurrent pains in the stump all his life, and perhaps pretty bad ones; and he will always be a one-legged man.

When someone we love dies, we are no longer the same person we were before; some essential dimension is gone.

Yet paradoxically the lost person also lives on in us in many ways. One form of this shared life is a physical, genetic legacy. The Native American poet Joy Harjo tells about a friend who finally tracked down the father he never knew as a boy, only to discover that his father had died a few months earlier. She predicts that this friend will keep looking for his lost father even though the father lives even now in his son's smile, his muscles— and in the search itself. The search is, in fact, a passionate part of the lived relationship, as in our search for God.

The contemporary practice of organ transplants puts this truth in even starker relief. In February of 2001, Seattle's annual Mardi Gras celebration turned violent and ugly. An out-of-control crowd fatally beat a young man. Later that year, his mother met with five recipients of his organs, warmly declaring that the diverse group kept her son alive and present for her. Though the search for organ transplants has led to exploitation and oppression on the global scene, donating a loved one's organs often provides consolation for friends and relatives. If the world were composed of isolated entities, it would be hard to imagine how the salvation the young man killed during Mardi Gras gave to others is compatible with an individual, separate life beyond death. But in a universe where we continually give and receive from one another in ways that shape and reshape body, mind, and spirit, it is a very concrete expression of the fact that we are somehow both individual selves and members of one body.

When the Saints Come Marching In

Aware of the links that connect everything in the cosmos, we can make better sense of another aspect of traditional pictures of paradise: the saints. I grew up in a world densely populated with saints. Statues, litanies, holy cards, feast days, and *Lives of the Saints* served as daily reminders of their virtues. These icons of holiness—Catherine, Teresa, Joseph, Jude—were not only models for how I should conduct myself; they could be mobilized to help with life's challenges, especially hopeless or desperate cases. The presence of saints instilled in me a sense that Earth and heaven are part of one unbroken circle. Long before quantum physics taught me about an interrelated universe, I considered myself part of a lively communion among the living and the dead.

Later I learned the dark side of saints. Their patronage supported a pyramid of power, making it necessary for those ranked farther from God's throne to have someone plead their cause. Saints were canonized for purely economic or political motives in this world, corrupting and distorting the meaning of holiness. They were also trivialized, called on once too often to locate a parking place or win a football game. The lives of the saints were also whitewashed, turned into tales of perfection impossible to emulate, or cautionary stories of obedience and humility that served the goals of the powerful in oppressing whole groups of people.

But saints are resilient, and they are making a comeback. Cleansed of their excesses and distortions, they are again able to strengthen connections between the generations, show us tangible models of holiness, and provide companionship in life's struggles. No longer up above us in some hierarchy of spiritual powers, saints are now all around us in a mutual exchange of encouragement and support. Not restricted to those canonized by official religions, they include a wide array of the living and dead who are recognized as having responded to grace in ways that furnish guidance and courage. Theologian Elizabeth A. Johnson uses an apt phrase to describe these people from all faiths, races, genders, and walks of life. She calls them "friends of God and prophets," drawing on a metaphor from the biblical Book of Wisdom.

The way of the saints is open to all of us, but some persons are grasped by grace so strongly that they focus their lives completely on this vision. There are countless examples of these persons through whom the Light shines: Mother Teresa's work with the dying and destitute gives her power in life and in death to inspire others. Oscar Romero's courage lives on with the force of resurrection in his Salvadoran people. Rosa Parks's refusal to relinquish her seat on a bus in 1955 inspires others not to submit to, or condone, racism.

So it makes sense to pray to saints and ancestors, to ask help from spouses and friends who have died. Such prayer affirms that they are present, that honoring their memory and imitating their lives brings the whole cosmos to a holiness none of us could find alone. Not only does such prayer change us, but the entire web of relationships is also transformed. We are all sustained by flows of energy and information that are deeper and broader than our conscious grasp. Praying to those who have died introduces new vitality and blessing into the circle of life. Moreover, when we understand that God is not an unmoved mover, but responsive Love, it becomes clear that these prayers are taken up into the divine life itself and given back to the world.

FOR PRAYER AND REFLECTION

For All the Saints: A Litany

A litany is a form of common prayer that strengthens the connections between the living and the dead. It originated in fourth-century Eastern Christianity from the prayer of the laity. It may take many forms, and the refrain varies: for example, "Pray for us," "Be with us," "Pray with us."

Participants may want to hold lighted candles.

The following is one suggested format, with a sampling of saints.

Leader: We gather in prayer to you, O God, with all the saints. May their lives hearten and strengthen us.

Leader: Sarah and Abraham, adventurers for God.

All: Be with us.

Leader: Mary Magdalene, witness to Resurrection.

All: Be with us.

Leader: Martin Luther, leader of reform.

All: Be with us.

Leader: Hildegard of Bingen, creator of sacred music.

All: Be with us.

Leader: Dietrich Bonhoeffer, martyr for truth.

All: Be with us.

Leader: Rachel Carson, lover of the Earth.

All: Be with us.

Leader: Mahatma Gandhi, advocate for nonviolence.

All: Be with us.

Leader: Dorothy Day, friend of the homeless.

All: Be with us.

(Pause for participants to name others who have influenced or inspired them.)

Leader: All you who have gone before us in life and in death, abide with us, and give us your spirit.

—Kathleen Fischer

May the angels lead you into Paradise:
may the martyrs come to welcome you—
and take you to the holy city,
the new and eternal Jerusalem.

—Recessional from the Roman Catholic Funeral Rite

7. Kinds of Presence

We meet the living dead....
in faith, hope, and love, that is,
when we open our hearts to the silent
calm of God's own self, in which they
live.

—Karl Rahner

*I*t is two years since my sister died of a brain tumor. The cancer was swift and relentless, and she lived only three months beyond the diagnosis. During her last days, several of us kept vigil at her bedside. The night she died, her hospice nurse had suggested that she might finally be able to let go if there were less activity in the house. So we left her with her husband. My younger sister and I had just arrived home and were getting ready for bed when the call came that she was gone. We drove back to her house through the cool, moonlit May night.

My niece wanted to be the one to dress her mother for her coffin, and she had spent a day carefully selecting her mother's favorite clothes. These included a warm red winter coat. She tucked pictures of those my sister loved into its pockets. She could not stand to think of her mother being alone and cold as she was lowered into the ground for her final journey. As we helped my niece, my younger sister sat for a time quietly holding our dear sister's feet. Then she looked up at me and said, "I'm thinking of your question, 'Where are you?'"

Months earlier I had remarked that, in doing grief work, I found my clients struggling with how to relate to a loved one who has died. After her brother was killed in a terrible car accident, a woman told me: "I want to shout, 'I don't know where you are!'" The questioning moves through many phases. First there is the sudden loss of all the ways this person has been present with us. The face, hands, and voice, once so familiar, are gone. The person seems to have simply disappeared. This creates, for many people, a nearly unbearable void. "Where are you?" becomes the cry of the heart.

Death as Absence and Presence

In her memoir *No Return Address*, Anca Vlasopolos tells how she carries her mother's ashes through German customs and over the ocean to Israel's shore. Her mother had told Anca more than once that, though she could not live in Israel, she would like to be dead there. Surely, Anca muses, her mother does not live in the orange grove in Israel where her ashes are now scattered. Yet she realizes that the fragrant orchard and the thin strip of sea visible from the hill make her feel as if something of what her mother cherished continues. Likewise, it is as if the consoling proximity of the grave of Anca's cousin in the cemetery nearby keeps her mother from being too lonely.

Many can identify with Anca's tangled knot of absence and presence, doubt and intuition, as she deals with her mother's death. One man I counseled kept going back to the moment when his wife's spirit seemed to leave her body.

I could not believe that someone who had been with me for over fifty years could just vanish. I have no sense of her being here, because I am still so aware of her "not here," her not being with me anymore.

Another woman began almost immediately to relate in a new way to her mother who had died.

I talk to mom all the time, asking her what I should do. Yesterday there was a beautiful rainbow in the sky and I knew she was with me.

Still another says,

I like having my grandmother's ashes in water. I can be near her in water everywhere. I have no trouble believing in a person's ongoing existence. I can't touch or see them, that's all. But they are present.

No single pattern fits everyone. But the desire to get in touch with the world beyond is widespread and longstanding. The question "Where are those who have died?" is pressing because it concerns our communion with all who have lived before us, and all who will exist after us. It tells us how we are to live not only in their absence, but also in their presence. Unless we will see our loved ones again, what could a redeemed world possibly mean?

Word From the Other Side

It is this desire to be in contact with the spirits of the dead that gives rise to spiritualist religion, whose pastors are called mediums. This religion's key ritual is the séance, in which revelations are sought from the dead. Even Christians have founded spiritualist churches to show that there is life after death, and thus prove that their religion is true. It is their attempt to defend religion against the onslaughts of science.

Although I share the desire to preserve belief in life after death, I am uneasy with spiritualism's efforts to subject the dead to our definitions of space and time, bending them to our questions and answers. That kind of exactitude reduces the mystery inherent in any understanding of the afterlife. I am also troubled by the way mediums can exploit persons in deep grief.

There is a different kind of knowing, one that could be called personal rather than scientific. It emphasizes the participation of the knower in a living process that is often intuitive and contextual, dependent upon previous experience. This way of knowing is less appreciated by science, but is nonetheless as important as knowledge that is public and objectively verifiable. It is more elusive, less marked by control and precision. It usually comes unbidden, and would be meaningless to a detached observer.

This kind of knowing fits the experiences that many people— relatives, friends, and clients—have shared with me. A friend awakens to see her dead sister standing at the foot of her bed, now no longer contorted and wasted with disease. A young man's father appears in a dream to say, "Don't worry about me. I'm fine, really, I am." An eighty-year-old widow is doing grief work. It is now nearly two years since her husband's death, and she is congratulating herself on making it through another Christmas. When I ask how it is going, she replies: "Not as bad. You know, I sense Greg is with me, looking after me. He's taking care of me the way he always did. It's not that he says anything. You know, Greg was never a big talker anyway. But I just know he is there, urging me on. I'll realize that he wants me to do something, and I find myself saying, "Yes, I know, I've got to get going."

The poet Rita Rainsford Rouner gives a more detailed description of this process of finding abiding relationship after loss. In *A Short While towards the Sun,* she comments on the series of poems she wrote while trying to connect her son's death to her own continuing life. Her son, Tim, died in August of 1977 in a mountain-climbing accident in Alaska. He was nineteen. Rouner says that in rereading her poems about Timmy she can see the variety of images that represent his living presence in her world: "The wide-eyed heart running to meet the day," "The incandescent boy," "My leggy colt leaping through shimmering grass." These and other images of eager engagement with the world suggest a sharpened awareness, and the enlarging of Rouner's own world through a connection to her child.

As Rouner abides in the midst of loss and separation, she becomes aware of other images as well. From the beginning, her experience of Timmy's death has included words of enduring connection. This is true of her earliest poem, which describes the accident. Rouner says that it arrived complete, as though it were a direct message from Tim about his experience of falling to his death. She calls it, "Into the Bright Immensities."

The fall was fatal.
The towering summit soared
into the glowing sky
and the lower face dropped away
in shadowed ridges.
You slid swiftly down the snowy slope
and tumbled off into the vibrant air,
crashing like a cataract
upon the ledge below.
Leaving your ruined young body,
a crystal pitcher in shattered pieces,
you pranced off into the enormous spaces
waiting to receive you.
The evening brimmed the world with radiance.
On the dark ledge your forsaken brother,
raging with grief
drenched your dead face
with tears and kisses;
while you, altered but whole,
romped up the sunlit peak
to stride the spired skyline
and dance upon the pinnacles,
laughing and throwing back kisses
and shouting down the splendors of the view.

Rouner finds herself deeply grateful for the gift of this portrait of her son in his death and resurrection. In it she recognizes qualities characteristic of him: vitality, responsiveness, a readiness to share.

Through her poetry, Rouner shows how it is possible to have an ongoing relationship with a loved one who has died. Death does not destroy the reality of a relationship; rather, the person remains present in our lives as a living being. The connection is constantly changing. Her own experience is grounded in Christian faith. She is drawn to the Gospel passage that assures us God holds in safekeeping even the sparrow that falls from the tree. She believes the continuing relationship with someone who has died is an experience of ongoing presence; it witnesses to God's power to preserve the bonds of love forever.

In the Embrace of God

In Latin American base communities, when the names of "the disappeared" and the martyrs are read, those gathered for worship respond, *"Presente."* Those named are present here with us in fellowship. The way the dead continue to be in our lives has been called a "second presence." That is, they are now free, and they leave us free. We do not have to suppress our memory of them in order to get on with our lives. Communities draw courage and hope from their ongoing presence.

Many biblical passages tell us that those who have died live on in God. But it does not always occur to us that God is where we are, and so our loved ones are with us too.

For I am convinced that neither death, nor life, nor angels, nor rulers, nor things present, nor things to come, nor powers, nor height, nor depth, nor anything else in all creation, will be able to separate us from the love of God in Christ Jesus our Lord. (Rom 8:38–39)

Whether we live or die, Paul says, we abide together in the great sea of God's love.

FOR PRAYER AND REFLECTION

Taking In the Love, Energy, and Prayers of Others

Take some time to imagine and bring to mind all those who have been and are continuing to send you thoughts, love, energy, and prayers. Let these all come into your being and move fully through you. Feel yourself encircled by them. Let yourself float on this gathering of love and prayers. When your courage, hope, and energy falter, return to this place and be borne up by the love of others who are remembering you.

—Kathleen Fischer

Comfort Shawls

Two women in Hartford, Connecticut, started the practice of knitting shawls to give to people who are grieving, suffering from illness, or celebrating an event. Whether called comfort, healing, prayer, or friendship shawls, they wrap a person in the prayers and support of others. Knitting them is itself a spiritual process, a gift of oneself, and an opportunity to pray and reflect. Women sometimes gather in groups to knit. They light a candle and pray that the recipient will receive comfort and strength from the shawl. Some knitters pass around their shawls so that others can stitch in a row that will symbolize the collective care woven into each shawl.

8. One With the Universe

dirt, mud, stars, water—
I know you as if you were myself.

How could I be afraid?
—Mary Oliver

n her memoir *Reason for Hope*, Jane Goodall tells about the solitude she experienced in the forests of Gombe. During sojourns there she knew moments of intense awareness of beauty and eternity. They came rarely and unannounced. At these times, inanimate objects developed their own identities for this scientist of chimpanzees. Like a transplanted St. Francis of Assisi, she found herself saying good morning to the peaks and the stream, and chastising the wind for howling overhead. She was drawn to the sound of the rain dropping on leaves, the intensely bright moonlight, and the fragrance of the white night flowers.

On one occasion, Goodall slipped into a state of heightened awareness. Later she struggled to find words for the experience. It seemed to her that *self* was completely absent, that she, along with the chimpanzees, earth, trees, and air, had become one with the spirit of life itself. There were new frequencies in the evensong of birds, amazingly high and sweet notes from the singing insects, an intense awareness of the color and pattern of leaves. Startled out of this moment by a distant chorus of pant-hoots and a chimp's reply, Goodall realized that she was in a sacred place.

Time in the forest increased the deep reverence Goodall already had for all life forms. The chimpanzees, the birds and insects, the waters of the lake, and the stars and planets formed for her one whole, one great mystery of which she was a part. Returned to England, she found it difficult to sense the presence of God. She had not yet learned, she said, to hold the peace of the forest within her.

Goodall's experience of being one with the sacred Depths of the universe is a brief foretaste of what we anticipate in life after death. Early in Christian thought, in the writings of Irenaeus, we find the view that the divinization, or union, of Creation with God is our destiny. Mystics of every time and place, including those who do not think they deserve that designation, have moments of such union. The experience also comes in ways less intense than Goodall's, like the quiet grace that accompanies attempts to contemplate, and care for, Creation.

I experienced this during a recent project to create a native habitat near our home in Seattle. Just now, amid wild rosebushes and alders, a red-winged blackbird announces spring. He and his companions have only recently returned to our block. Until our group of volunteers, backed by a city grant, reclaimed it, his home was a vacant lot disfigured by weeds, garbage, and vandalism. Our contemplation takes the form of weeding, mulching, and planting. Oregon grape, mock orange, snowberry, and thimbleberry now flourish. A blue heron swoops over our heads during winter work. Five ducklings emerge from a mallard's nest, snuggled among cattails and reeds. Here, like Goodall in Gombe, I experience a unity with all beings. Joined to the Source of Creation, I am less afraid of death, or life.

New understandings of the cosmos provide fresh underpinnings for such experiences and their meaning for life beyond death.

Belonging Fully to the Universe

At her grandmother's funeral, a ten-year-old girl worked up the courage to ask her pastor: "Where do you think Granny is now?" Her pastor replied: "I can't tell you exactly, but I'm certain she's somehow with us in this universe."

One way to expand this pastor's intuition is to reflect on death as a return to the Divine Matrix. A matrix is the place or point from which something originates. For example, we say that the Greco-Roman world was the matrix for Western civilization. The earliest meaning of *matrix* is "the womb." It is thus a good term for matter at the subatomic level. There the classical distinction between matter and energy no longer exists; matter is clustered energy, and energy is the field of the interconnections throughout the entire universe. This dancing void of matter/energy is pregnant with promise. Like the fecundity of a womb, it is waiting to give birth in unpredictable ways.

When we talk about the Divine Matrix, we mean the nourishing Life Force from which all creatures arise. It is the Holy as a generous, fertile source of energy. It is Divine Spirit as the hidden well of creativity giving birth to asteroids, rocks, bald eagles, ponderosa pines, women and men. The same energy that first birthed the universe is active now, blossoming not only into our planet and galaxies, but also into us, our families, and all other beings. One way to envision the afterlife, then, is as a return to this originating Source of all things, the Love from which life arises, perhaps to keep breaking forth in new forms and combinations.

Although it is helpful to envision our final union with the universe as a return to the Divine Matrix, the notion of a matrix can seem abstract. For that reason I like the more personal language used in conversations between scientist Fritjof Capra and theologian David Steindl-Rast. Their theme is "belonging to the universe." For them the sense of connectedness with the whole cosmos is the quintessence of religious experience. It means feeling that I am intimately related to a reality much greater than myself.

It is realizing that the smile of any baby, or even of a dolphin, is also somehow my smile. They know that human beings often feel lost and at sea, wandering and searching for something. But certain religious experiences lay bare the fact that we are not alone and adrift, we belong to all other humans, to all the animals, to all the plants. We simply fail to realize it. I am responsible to them and they to me. We all belong together to a great cosmic unity. When we say, "I belong," we mean "Here I find my place," "This is it." The realization that our home is the cosmos, the sense of belonging in this way, is salvation. It is the redemption we seek when we dream of life after death. And it starts now.

Can We Still Be Ourselves?

Among those who view the afterlife as a return to the Source that birthed us, there is disagreement on a key question. When we re-enter this cosmic womb at death, do we lose our identity? Some see the end of life as absorption into the Cosmic Matrix. Many find this enough. It is this Matrix that is everlasting, not individual beings. Death is a natural phase of the life cycle. In death we release our bodies and minds to the power at the heart of the universe from which new beings continuously arise.

Such is the position, for instance, of theologian Rosemary Ruether. She reminds us that throughout life we can either poison the well of life by diminishing other beings, or we can dance gracefully with them, affirming their creative work as well as our own. She envisions us surrendering our small selves back into the great Self at death, confident of our contribution to the larger community. Then when we surrender to the Matrix of Life, it will be with an ultimate trust: "Mother, into your hands I commend my spirit. Use me as you will in your infinite creativity."

Others believe this final union will make us more, not less, uniquely ourselves. Our unity with all beings is even now increasingly apparent to us, and yet there is no question of our uniqueness. Nature is like a vast ocean from which new wonders continually bubble up. Decades ago, the paleontologist and religious thinker Teilhard de Chardin insisted that true union differentiates. Like all genuine love, it does not swallow up uniqueness, but enhances it. A striking example of this for me is the recently budding bright-colored passionflower that no one had seen bloom since the nineteenth century. Its flowers will live about one day before they close. An expert on this *Passiflora* believes the temperature, daily sunlight, height of its vines, age of the plant, and amount of rain have to be aligned perfectly for it to bloom. Such is its interdependence with its ecology. Like an embryo it exchanges energy with its environment, yet it remains in a class by itself. Apparently, for over a hundred years, the conditions were not quite right for its blooming.

We arise from the Matrix, live creatively from what we receive, and are woven back into it. Yet all along we experience our connection to God and other beings as an interpersonal dialogue. We call God Companion and Friend to us as well as to all Creation. Why should the dialogue not continue beyond death? When we use the metaphor of Trinity to refer to God, we are saying that even the Divine Reality is at once one and many. Cannot we, too, return to God and yet maintain our own selfhood?

Process theologian Marjorie Suchocki thinks so. She describes the resurrection of the world into the divine life as a stretching out from our personal center to other personal centers. In her vision of the cosmic dance, each element of the universe is fully itself yet a participant in divine life. Thus, though final union need not mean total absorption into the whole, what does disappear is the illusion that we exist in isolated worlds. At times even now we get a taste of the unity that is possible among selves. It is that full-blown unity that we hope for.

Danah Zohar describes such a personal experience in *The Quantum Self*. Throughout her book Zohar probes modern physics for insights into what it might mean for us to relate to one another. She ponders whether there is a subatomic wellspring that is the origin of creativity, empathy with others, and feelings of unity with the inanimate world. She has planned all along to address the question of immortality in her book, but she realizes that, for some reason, she never seems to get to it. Meanwhile, she is pregnant with her first child, and somehow loses her lifelong terror of death. She becomes bodily aware of herself as part of a larger process. Her sense of herself as an isolated individual gets shaken up. She experiences herself as extending inward toward unlimited possibility and outward toward all life. What results is a whole new way of envisioning the survival of the self. And now she can write her chapter on immortality.

Artists and poets continue to imagine how union of the one and the many is possible, aiding our imaginations as we ponder the question. In her memoir *The Stations of Still Creek*, Barbara Scot muses on the illness and death of a dear friend. There comes to her the image of him stepping off a bluff edge, not into a canyon, "but into some vast, interstellar space of snowflake ashes, liberated for recombination."

Do Ho Suh, a Korean sculptor, keeps exploring in his works the complex relationship between individual and corporate identity. His stunning creations suggest that we have only begun to plumb the topic. Even the titles of Suh's works shake up our grammar: *Some/One* and *Who Am We?*

In this latter piece, which is done with four colors of print on paper, Suh creates an unstructured whole out of thousands of tiny photographs taken from his high school yearbook. At a distance, his work looks like an abstract design. Upon closer inspection, the pattern reveals itself to be individual faces, each clearly defined by the physical characteristics of a particular classmate. The only limitation of this work for our present purposes is that it is static, while the creative energy of the Divine Matrix is dancing, surging, ever bringing forth fresh creations.

FOR PRAYER AND REFLECTION

In Praise of Creation

Divine Artist,
We praise you
for the humble song sparrow
making endlessly varied melodies
with whole-bodied vigor;

for ancient red cedars
guarding sanctuaries of stillness;

for purple saxifrage
flowering sturdily amid Arctic ice;

for jewel scarabs, brilliant beetles
raining color on Honduran forests;

for the sea's seasons,
wild winds and crashing waves,
gentle tide pools harboring myriad forms;

for a global rainbow of persons,
rooted in one earth
yet enigmatically different,
each bearing an image of you.

Thank you for a universe so transparent to your beauty.
In life and in death, we trust in your boundless creative love.

—Kathleen Fischer

Do not stand at my grave and weep
I am not there. I do not sleep.

I am a thousand winds that blow.
I am the diamond glint on snow.

I am the sunlight on ripened grain.
I am the gentle autumn rain.

When you wake in the morning hush
I am the swift, uplifting rush
of quiet birds in circling flight.
I am the soft starlight at night.

Do not stand at my grave and weep.
I am not there. I do not sleep.

—Joyce Fossen

9. Remembrance

When the thing we freely forfeit is kept
with fonder a care,
Fonder a care kept than we could have kept it.
—Gerard Manley Hopkins

or days after the September 11 attack on the World Trade Center in New York, people here in Washington State carried flowers to the Seattle Center Fountain, a large gathering place in the center of the city. A memorial intended to last a few hours just kept growing. In the end there were a million blossoms. We felt somehow joined with those who had died, and with those who grieved them, whether we knew them personally or not. Even on the first anniversary of the attack, Mozart's *Requiem* was performed here to a large audience, as it was in countless places around the globe, in musical solidarity with those who had died.

Remembrance is linked to death in multiple ways. The love or hate we offer the world continues to reverberate throughout the cosmos. Those we have loved live on in us, and we in them, in memory, among other ways. God, too, holds us in memory. Each of these forms of remembrance connects this world with the next.

We Will Never Forget You

After working in nursing homes for nearly a decade, I began reading the daily obituary notices on a regular basis. I wanted to know when one of the residents died. Over the years I have continued this practice, not now to learn of the death of a former client, but simply because the death notices provide such a perspective on human life and death. Obituaries summarize an individual's halting attempts to make something meaningful of one limited lifespan. They set aside for the moment a person's flaws and failures, and concentrate on positive qualities and lasting legacies.

According to these notices, people are grateful not only for others' contributions to family and friends, but also for what they gave to justice, science, art, education, medicine, and church. We find as well an accounting of someone's simple joys: music, singing, tennis, cooking, collie dogs, bird watching, bridge, travel. There is appreciation for a person's unique gifts: wit, joy in simple pleasures, honesty, love of nature, kind words, courage in illness, love of family and friends. "He could make you feel at home with just a hello," one notice says. And another, "When she came into your home, everybody immediately felt more peaceful."

Obituary columns also contain many familiar metaphors for heaven. The dead are in the hands of God, will shine like bright stars, are finally at peace, have been raised to new life, have joined family in a heavenly reunion, will no longer suffer, have wiped away all tears. One theme recurs in these brief entries: Determination that the person not be forgotten. As one puts it, "His spirit and energy live on in his family and in the lives of all who knew him." A young classmate declares of an eight-year-old friend who died: "She is in my heart and your heart. She is still with us." We understand that our atoms and genes survive, but there is more to it than that. All that we have personally inserted into the universe is still in the mix. Our choices have permanent significance. We help create the future, all the way to eternity.

Together Though Separated

In *The Pleasure of Their Company*, Dolores Grumbach talks about planning a party for her eightieth birthday. She looks through her address book to find friends to invite. The names are all there, but many are no longer living. She muses on how, as we grow older, the people we love who have died sometimes have vitality greater than the living. They suddenly leap to life when she least expects it. Grumbach dismisses the truism that we must have some kind of closure in order to find peace after the death of a loved one. As for her, she says, she prefers no closure. It allows the dead to reside permanently in her memory, outside time and place.

Among the dead with whom she still keeps company is Dorothy Day, the founder of the Catholic Worker Movement. Grumbach first met her when, as a college student, she visited Dorothy's hospitality house in the slums of Little Italy. She recalls washing dishes with her on the two days she had free of classes each week, and noticing that Dorothy's arms were covered with red marks. Dorothy explained that they came from bedbugs. For her, Grumbach says, Dorothy still lives, without halo, handing out doughnuts and coffee and scratching the red lumps on her arms.

But death does mean separation. How can memory connect us with those we have lost? Contemporary science revolutionizes not only how we view space and time, but also how we understand our relationships with others. Quantum physics tells us that once two entities have interacted with one another, no matter how far apart they then move, they retain the capacity to mutually influence one another. We can no longer think of individuals as simply isolated bits and pieces. Life is an interconnected field. No ultimate division in space or time exists among individual beings. I am literally and physically a part of others' becoming, and they are a part of mine.

Which brings us back to memory. Memory is a form of presence, and the degree of presence depends on how fully others inhabit my being. We are frequently more present to someone at a distance than to those next to us in the same room. Take a student who has just fallen in love. My classroom experience leaves me no doubt that he is much more fully present to his lover in Kansas than to me at the podium, though only fifteen feet separate us.

Memory, as understood in quantum physics, is not simply the recollection of facts and experiences. It is *live* connection, a *lived* dialogue with the past. The past exists not as a finished reality that I may or may not be able to recall. Rather it is a presence that continues to define me. This is the physical basis of ritual, of memorials such as Passover meals and eucharistic celebrations, of birthday parties and funeral liturgies. Through ritual we enliven the past and integrate it more fully into present experience.

The present can also give the past new life and meaning, and sometimes transform it entirely. The clearest example I know of this is the healing that my clients are able to complete with someone who has died. One woman finds herself surprised at how positively she now thinks of her deceased parents. It is different, she says, from other stages of life when she was determined she was not going to be like them at all. In her words: "Now I can't go to a baseball game without thinking of my father. That's the one thing we did together when I was growing up. When I look at my hands I see my mother's hands. I can now admit that she was an incredibly neat lady—strong and intelligent along with being very sad and depressed. It's like I've absorbed their identities and affirmed who they are as human beings. I wonder if that's what it means to have someone live on in you." She concludes by saying that this awareness is not sad anymore, but pleasant. There is a new companionship.

Ritual as a Form of Remembrance

In her quietly elegant novel *The Samurai's Garden*, Gail Tsukiyama describes the yearly pilgrimage to honor ancestors during the Ghosts' Feast. Matsu and his sister Fumiko, like the other people of the small Japanese village of Tarumi, have been up for hours preparing food to bring to the graves of their ancestors. On the kitchen table are bowls of pickled vegetables, deep-fried tofu, rice balls filled with beans, and salted fish. Matsu, Fumiko, and the novel's main character, the young Stephen, leave the house just as the sun rises. Many other villagers are already making their way down the dirt road with *furoshikis* filled with food for their ancestors.

The procession grows as it moves toward the temple and cemetery. When they arrive, Stephen notices how the gravestones in Tarumi are plain and simply engraved. Many of those in Hong Kong, where he has often made the yearly pilgrimage, are more elaborate and contain small photos of the deceased embedded in stone. "I had always enjoyed walking slowly down the crooked rows of gravestones," he says, "somehow moved by the faces staring back at me. They were images of youth and glamour, age and wisdom. It didn't matter. I walked away each year taking these faces with me, as if in that short time I had somehow come to know them."

Many traditions have rituals for honoring the dead. Deceased relatives and friends are remembered every November in the Catholic liturgy for All Soul's Day. On *Dia de los Muertos*, the Day of the Dead, Mexicans erect altars with photos and mementos of their loved ones. They have picnic lunches in cemeteries. They are unafraid to be among the dead and reconnect in a livelier way with deceased loved ones through this active, ritual remembrance.

In Celtic lore also, there is a strong conviction that the dead are not far away. The Irish tradition holds that this world and the eternal world are interwoven. Often as a person is dying, he or she sees a deceased grandparent, parent, spouse, or friend. The veil between the two worlds is very thin now, and friends from the eternal world come to take a person home. The holy water sprinkled around the body of the dead person drives away the dark forces and holds the person in light as they make their final journey. In Ireland there is also the tradition called *caoineadh*. These are the people, usually women, who come to mourn the dead person. With high-pitched wailing they tell the story of the person's life, a sad and beautiful gathering of key events, a narrative filled with the immense loneliness of loss.

We sometimes too lightly discard these crucial rituals. In a culture built on individualism, a widow laments that her children do not understand why she wants to visit her husband's grave: "They tell me it's just a corpse. Well, I *know* that! But going there—it's a symbol, a movement, a grace. It's a memory." Though we may not return to established rituals, we do need concrete ways to remember. Memorial objects and ritual actions retain their power to strengthen bonds and to heal them.

Held in God's Memory

For the ancient Hebrew, the ultimate loss was to be forgotten, erased from the memory of family and tribe, and from the memory of God. If God forgets you, you might as well have never existed. It is the ultimate disaster. When exiled Israel fears God has abandoned her, the prophet Isaiah insists that God remembers her everlastingly.

Can a woman forget her nursing
child,
or show no compassion for the
child of her womb?
Even these may forget,
yet I will not forget you. (49:15)

Contemporary process thought, chiefly indebted to Alfred North Whitehead, uses this concept of divine remembrance to explain how we survive death. Process thought sees God not as a changeless and distant being, but as someone in constant dialogue with the world. Not only does God make a difference to us, but we also make a difference to God. God has a real relationship with Creation, and knows every reality precisely as it experienced itself: its sorrows and joys, triumphs and failures.

God, whom in this context Whitehead calls "Final Wisdom," holds fast all that in our experience has now moved beyond the present moment. Our lives are continually taken up into the divine, and in light of them, redemptive possibilities are offered back to the world. Over and against the waste and tragedy in life, a renewing power is also ever at work. The future will embody our efforts, along with God's, even if its particular shape is not what we anticipate. Our endeavors may, in fact, be used in totally unexpected ways. The poet Marilyn Nelson captures this possibility in her sequence of poems *Mama's Promises*. She pictures God as a nourishing mother who says:

> I want to be remembered
> with a dark face absorbing all colors
> and giving them back twice as brightly,
> like water remembering light.

Not only is the past preserved in God, it is transformed. God's tender care and infinite patience act to see that nothing is lost that can be salvaged, even what the world might consider "mere wreckage." And divine remembrance, because it redeems, includes a measure of forgetting: "For I will forgive their iniquity, and remember their sin no more" (Jer 31:34). Whitehead says that God preserves what is worth preserving; what is trivial is relegated to triviality.

As each moment of our existence is transfigured in the divine life, it thus takes on permanent significance. God receives it in all its uniqueness and individuality. This everlasting reality is what Whitehead understands by the "kingdom of heaven." In spite of the waste in the world, the past is not finally lost. We contribute not only to our own and others' enjoyment, but even everlastingly to the joy of God.

FOR PRAYER AND REFLECTION

The Ritual of Candle Lighting

Lighting a candle is a simple ritual of remembrance. Let its flame sustain you in awareness of the Holy. Let it remind you of those persons, living or dead, whom you are holding in prayer and remembrance.

—Kathleen Fischer

For Those Who Have Died

In the ten thousand flowers of spring,
the blue sky, the breeze of summer,
we will remember you.

In the harvest moon,
the fierce rain,
the snow of winter,
we will remember you.

When we are afraid and lonely,
sick or suffering,
we will remember you.

In laughter and joy,
love and beauty,
we will remember you.

We honor your memory always,
for you live on in us.

May you be held
in the warm embrace
of the One whose remembrance is everlasting.

—Kathleen Fischer

10. Meeting the Light

...the whole fabric of creation is woven
through with the thread of God's light. It
is like a material shot through with silk.
If somehow this thread were removed the whole
of creation would unravel.

— J. Philip Newell

he Oglala Sioux have a practice of gathering just before dawn to welcome the morning star. This is especially important when there has been a recent death in the community, as well as at other times of crisis. The darkest time of night occurs just before the dawn breaks, and the daybreak star signifies wisdom and renewal. As the colors of a new day appear on the horizon, promise and possibility return as well.

Other creatures also usher in the dawn. The research scientist Alexandra Morton, while documenting the mysteries of whale intelligence, photographed the orcas Corky and Orky greeting the sun each morning. They did this by pinpointing, with blow-hole spray and licks, the exact spot where the sun struck their tank walls. The rising sun is a constant reminder of the creative Spirit that dwells within the universe.

Not just the dawn, but light itself is a familiar symbol of the sacred. Biblical writers, from the prophet Isaiah to John the Evangelist, speak of the brightness of God's coming, of God as the light of life. Mystics describe the blinding radiance of meeting the Mystery. In Gothic cathedrals, stained glass windows make light tangible. Though light reveals reality, it is itself difficult to grasp. We cannot stare into the light, nor can we fully apprehend its origin. Even scientific studies of light fail to penetrate its mystery. We are only now able to see the light emanating from the birth of the universe billions of years ago.

Many of us encounter light as a divine epiphany in ordinary times and places. An old growth grove in one of the Pacific Northwest's ancient forests is such a spot for me. A dense canopy of majestic fir, cedar, pine, spruce, and hemlock trees blankets the area, making it quite dark on a cloudy day. But on sunny days, light breaks in at various places. It highlights branches, leaves, and needles. Unnoticed before, they momentarily take center stage, beautiful in the glistening sun. As the intensity of the light increases, additional aspects of the forest are revealed.

Light is also a common symbol for paradise. Hopeful depictions of life after death promise that the small shafts of light we experience now will someday flare into full radiance. In hell, in contrast, there is utter darkness. The poet Dante called it a place "mute of all light." If God's light is the heart and center of Creation, then living in the light becomes an apt way to speak of union with the Mystery. Luminous moments in life offer glimpses into what the afterlife might be like.

Reports of Light in Near-Death Experiences

In 1975 Raymond Moody published his depiction of near-death experiences, *Life After Life*. While in medical school, Moody, who was a philosophy professor before becoming a psychiatrist, began collecting accounts of these occurrences. Based on one hundred fifty stories, he developed a description of a typical near-death experience. Moody's book became a bestseller, and today debates about the topic continue in numerous books, articles, and films.

Many people report having had near-death experiences, and there are common features in their testimonies. Carol Zaleski, who has extensively researched these accounts in both medieval and modern times, identifies the following elements.

1. Separation from the body, with the persons sometimes watching the scene from a distant vantage point; for example, observing medical efforts to resuscitate them.
2. A journey-experience, such as moving through a dark tunnel toward a source of light.
3. Meeting with deceased relatives or friends, or with a presence described as a kind of "being of light."
4. Some form of life review or remembering of past deeds.
5. An indescribable fullness of light and love, often accompanied by a sense of peace and safety.
6. The return to life to complete unfinished business.
7. Positive effects, which endure; for instance, release from the fear of death, a new energy for life, or a renewed commitment to love and service.

Although near-death testimonies differ, reflecting the religious and cultural beliefs of different historical periods, nearly all cultures have stories of persons who pass through death and return with messages for the living. The narratives are not meant simply to satisfy curiosity. They are stories of conversion, and their purpose is to communicate to others what their narrators have learned.

How are we to evaluate near-death experiences in relation to belief in an afterlife? They have limitations, of course, as do all images and narratives. The most fruitful approach seems to lie somewhere between the two extremes of totally dismissing them or of seeing them as unassailable evidence of life after death. Near-death testimonies do not empirically prove long-term survival. But they do intimate what happens in the first seconds or moments after clinical death. At the very least, they suggest that there is something more, another dimension to reality.

It is striking that the person reports seeing what is happening from a vantage point outside of his or her body. Senses sharpen and minds clear the moment they disengage from the body. For example, a survivor of anaphylactic shock recalls: "I was fully aware of what was happening both physically and in the minds of those in the emergency room until I was revived, at which point I was very confused." Though it is an out-of-body experience, it is not a dreamlike state. Near-death survivors say it is vivid and coherent, marked by the ability to deliberate and to assess their situation accurately. This suggests that consciousness can at least momentarily separate from the body.

References to light in these narratives are also instructive. Zaleski opens her detailed study *Otherworld Journeys* with two stories. The first is that of Tom Sawyer, a heavy-equipment operator from Rochester, New York. Tom describes the fifteen minutes in which he lay crushed under the weight of his pickup truck. He says that his heart had stopped and everything was completely black. Then the void took the shape of a tunnel and there was "the most magnificent light; it's The Light in capital letters, and it's—very bluntly—the essence of God."

The second account has been attributed to Salvius, a sixth-century holy man who, according to the *History of the Franks*, spent a night lifeless on a funeral bier but revived when God sent him back to serve the church as a bishop. Salvius says that, four days previously, he died and went to the height of heaven. It was as though he not only rose above the Earth, but even above the sun and moon, the clouds and stars. He then went through a gate that was brighter than normal daylight, into a place where the entire floor shone like gold and silver: "The light was indescribable, and I can't tell you how vast it was."

In both these accounts, drawn from very different historical periods, light is a symbol for the Holy. The presence of light in near-death narratives corresponds to, and is likely drawn from, imagery common to encounters with the divine in this life and beyond death. As is true of depictions of light in religious literature generally, this meeting with ultimate reality takes many forms. The light in near-death accounts might be a conversation with God, a meeting with an individual "being of light" such as Christ, or a surrounding presence filled with insight and love. Or it may include several of these features.

What We Know/What We Love

Something else of interest characterizes near-death testimonies. In both medieval and modern accounts, attempts to describe the light blend visual qualities with terms for emotion, such as warmth, peace, energy, and love. This mixture of imagery suggests that knowing and loving intersect. Not only does vision clear so that a person sees the beauty and importance of every aspect of reality. There is also a change in will and emotion that makes it possible to love every living being. This is different from trying to force ourselves to appreciate and love. Rather it is the gift of seeing ordinary things in a new light, in their true light. When that happens, we are moved to love.

Zaleski says that in her research on near-death accounts, she found this union of knowledge and love to be one of the few core elements that cut across different cultures and historical periods. It is, to use an overworked term, an experience of wholeness. No longer are a person's thoughts, desires, intellect, and will in conflict. There is the unity described by mystics of all persuasions. Persons know who they are and are meant to be. They grasp the truth and direction of life. They also feel greater compassion and joy than they have ever known.

The contemplative writer Thomas Merton speaks of his own initiation into this kind of seeing and loving. He says he was in Louisville in the midst of the shopping district at the intersection of Fourth and Walnut. Suddenly he was overwhelmed with the realization that he loved all these people bustling about him. For a moment his false sense of separateness lifted. He saw that, in the heart of God, he was one with all humanity. Writing about the experience later, Merton explains that there is a place at the center of our being that is untouched by the illusion of separateness. It is a point of nothingness where God dwells. He compares it to a pure diamond that blazes with heaven's invisible light. He believes that it is in everyone, and if we could see the convergence of all these billions of points of light, the flame would burn away the darkness and cruelty in the world. "I have no program for this seeing," Merton concludes. "It is only given. But the gate of heaven is everywhere."

One medieval depiction of this union of knowing and loving comes from the great poet of paradise, Dante Alighieri. Dante completed *The Divine Comedy* shortly before his death in 1321. In it, he travels through hell and purgatory, and is eventually granted permission to ascend through the various heavens all the way up to the highest heaven, or empyrean. Upon arrival there, Dante experiences the divine source of light and love.

For Dante, light is an apt image for the intangible and invisible. Light is virtually immaterial, without shape, color, taste, or smell. Yet it is visible as the source of visibility itself. For Dante, God is the blazing point at the center of the universe. Dante's guide, Beatrice, explains to him that the entire cosmos hangs from this Point, which both contains and exceeds all space and time. This flame is the force that fuses our fragmented powers. Like a wheel, God moves Dante's intellect and will, knowledge and love, forward on the axis of love.

> But already my desire and my will were revolved,
> like a wheel that is evenly moved,
> by the Love which moves the sun
> and the other stars.
> (30.143–145)

By desire, Dante means the desire of the intellect for a unifying vision. He experiences all that is scattered and separate in the universe as bound together in God's Love. For a brief moment he has a foretaste of the beatitude that awaits us all.

Dante's *Paradiso* is set within medieval cosmology. In that cosmos the Love of God directs the heavenly bodies like the sun and the stars musically in their orbits. God moves the universe as the reason for its existence. In our new cosmic story, the image of the divine Love binding all things together takes on fresh meaning. With Dante we can declare that our whole being finds direction in the same Love that moves the sun and stars. Finally to know the Beloved whom the universe desires, the Love which is its Ground, is paradise.

FOR PRAYER AND REFLECTION

A Meditation on Light

Take some time to increase your awareness of the sacredness of light, and the way God's light is the center of life.

Begin with some moments of silent openness to the Mystery, and this prayer from Psalm 36:9:

For with you is the fountain of
life;
in your light we see light.

As you pray the verse slowly, or repeat it as a mantra, call to mind some of your favorite images of light, and let each deepen within you.

These images may be:

- the light of dawn as darkness gives way to day
- the sun creating ribbons of light on water, or slowly setting as a ball of fire
- moonlight glancing off freshly fallen snow
- autumn light deepening the reds and golds of leaves
- shafts of light moving across fields or through trees
- stars brightening the night sky

When you have stayed for a while with the images that come to you, close with the psalm verse.

—Kathleen Fischer

In a passage from Daniel 12:1–3, a special reward is promised to those who make others wise. It is said that they shall be luminous beings, shining like the stars forever. A selection from Antoine de Saint-Exupéry's *The Little Prince* expresses that belief. It is especially helpful for family and friends of children who have died:

In one of the stars I shall be living.
In one of them I shall be laughing.
And so it will be as if all the stars were laughing,
When you look at the sky at night.

Part III

How Does Life Now Relate to Life Then?

11. Earth Crammed With Heaven

Earth's crammed with heaven,
And every common bush afire with God;
But only he who sees takes off his shoes;
The rest sit round it and pluck blackberries.
— Elizabeth Barrett Browning

n the months following the loss to cancer of three women who were clients of mine, I frequently caught myself staring up at the night sky. I searched the moon and stars like a farmer wanting some sign that a long drought was coming to an end. I cannot say exactly what I thought the skies would tell me, but they remained deeply silent. Perhaps I hoped these cherished women might be somewhere up there, and if I gazed long and hard enough I would see them again.

I had lost sight of what they had taught me, especially during their last months. They were very ill. Yet they loved this world and, in spite of nausea and weakness, terror and tears, they engaged life fully up to the very end. They donned outrageous hats to replace hair lost to chemotherapy, loved to the final minutes everything they were leaving behind, and trusted the Mystery they had known in this life to somehow sustain them through death.

In the spirit of these women I needed to look not up, but around me, for pieces of heaven right here on Earth. But to do that, I had to move beyond the religious notion that Earth is not our lasting home, and we are strangers here, awaiting a better country. Perhaps so. But look what this thinking does to our planet. We become tenants who trash furniture and scribble on walls, moving on without even paying a damage deposit. We destroy species, pollute streams, slash forests, for what do they matter anyway?

Yet when Moses encounters God in the blazing bush, he is told: "Remove the sandals from your feet, for the place on which you are standing is holy ground" (Exod 3:5). The Holy lies at the heart of Creation, and here fire is its symbol. The poet Gerard Manley Hopkins laments our blindness to the grandeur of God, flaming throughout the Creation: "nor can foot feel, being shod." In the city, where most of us live, concrete highways, shopping malls, and skyscrapers seem to obstruct our vision of this world as a sacred place. We cannot feel the rhythm of the sea, call the birds by name, nor hear their songs to their maker.

But if we cannot find the beginnings of heaven on Earth, we will continue to view this world as simply a vale of tears, a mere rest stop on the trip home, not the holy place in which the redemption of the entire cosmos begins. It helps to meditate on the many ways that Earth is crammed with heaven, on the wonder of the universe's intricacy, immensity, order, and novelty.

Intricacy

The poet Jane Kenyon died in April of 1995, after a fifteen-month struggle with leukemia. In her final days she and her husband finished a manuscript of her poems, later published as *Otherwise*. Her husband notes in his afterword that Kenyon lived in the shadow of depression, yet found joy in her body and in Creation, in wild asters and piano music, in paintings, hayfields, and her dog.

Light and darkness are never far apart in Kenyon's poems. Her effort to imagine redemption in the midst of suffering was constant, resulting in poetry of subtle grace, as in the opening lines of "Peonies at Dusk."

White peonies blooming along the porch
send out light
while the rest of the yard grows dim.

Poets hold fast to the Earth and reveal its details to be vessels of grace. They find the mystery of the whole in the particular — barn swallows and chrysanthemums, laughing children and gnarled elders. Every rose is on fire, no less than Moses' burning bush.

In the movie *Contact*, when the Pod launches Dr. Arroway into humanity's first meeting with non-earthlings, she suddenly realizes that true vision is the fusion of fact and faith. Mission Control pleads with her to describe what she sees. She can only reply: "They should have sent a poet." In their faithfulness to people and things, poets bring to mind the Buddhist belief that the eternal is realized in the *suchness* or *thisness* of each ordinary thing.

When poets are scientists as well, their expressions of wonder are replete with precise scientific information on the intricacies of the universe. This is the case with Chet Raymo, who in *Natural Prayers* writes about Earth's smallest marvels, unveiling both nature's beauty and its terror. Raymo asks us to contemplate the dragonfly. It has survived for more than three hundred million years with little change. Dragonflies come with many names: clubtails, darners, skimmers. They are skillful aviators with immense wingspans; large species can reach an air speed of sixty miles an hour. Iridescent, they light up the summer with shimmering blues and greens.

Or consider the spider. An ordinary garden spider can produce as many as eight kinds of silk — not only web silk, but those used for protecting eggs or binding prey. Experiments have shown that spider threads can be contracted to a twentieth of their length in the web without sagging, or stretched to three times their length without breaking. We can only marvel at these artists as the sunlight glances off their silky tapestries on household beams or doorways.

In *The Sacred Depth of the Universe*, the noted cell biologist Ursula Goodenough displays the amazing dynamics of biology. She starts with the cells that compose living creatures, taking us through the world of membranes, DNA, and proteins to describe in minute detail how life works. Even at this spare level, life has the beauty of a symphony. Goodenough espouses a religious naturalism; for her, nature encompasses all that is. But the origins and evolution of the universe evoke in her a sense of reverent wonder. Though she does not use the word *God* for the creative force that animates the universe, Goodenough is comfortable singing traditional hymns with her Presbyterian congregation, and addressing this Mystery in prayer. Nor does she need a promise of permanence to sustain her joy in the splendid particulars of the world. When she wonders what it will be like to be dead, she says she tells herself that it will be like before she was born.

Goodenough recounts the story of a young bonobo chimp that injured a bird while playing with it. The chimp picked up the comatose bird and carried it to the top of a tree. There she opened her hand. When the bird still lay limply in it, the chimp wrapped her legs around the tree trunk and held the bird by its wings. She then opened and closed the wings several times, apparently attempting to help the bird start to fly.

Immensity

In 1990 the space shuttle *Hubble* was launched. The images this ten-ton camera is returning are like nothing ever seen before. *Hubble* is able to capture things so far away in space and distant in time that its pictures are astonishing astronomers. This is the kind of celestial gazing that increases admiration, heightening the realization that Earth is the tiniest fragment of a much larger, longer story.

To start with the stars, we find that there are a hundred thousand million of them in our own little galaxy. According to one scientist's calculations, that is about twenty stars for each man, woman, and child on Earth. And there are more than a hundred thousand million galaxies. That is twenty galaxies for every man, woman, and child on Earth. The clusters and superclusters of galaxies lie at immense distances from us, some so far away that it takes nearly 12,000 million years for their light, traveling at 186,000 miles per second, to reach us.

In *Cosmos*, Brian Swimme suggests that we cannot grasp the marvel of these cosmic immensities through facts alone. We need to get out from under urban pollution to a place where we can lie on our backs and notice how the Milky Way runs from one horizon all the way down to the opposite side of the world. There we ponder that its light comes from the three hundred billion stars in the Milky Way Galaxy.

Scientists continue their celestial gazing, and new discoveries keep emerging. The more scientists see of Mars, for example, the more mystified they are by its terrain: "Some of the images were, aside from any scientific revelations, simply dazzling displays of nature's art: Byzantine dune-field sculptures, black scrawls etched by Martian dust devils." Jim Garvin, NASA's chief scientist for Mars exploration, says that when he first gazed at some of the images from the *Surveyor's* camera, he was moved to tears. There is nothing on Earth resembling many of Mars's features.

Order and Novelty

Mathematics discloses a hidden order embedded in the chaos churning around us. This leads some mathematicians to speak of their work as discovery, not invention. Music is woven into the very fabric of the spheres. We do not invent it; it displays its own melodies. Creation reveals a randomness that somehow has a structure, an order within topsy-turvy freedom. There is also a wonderful symmetry and simplicity to the world, an economic use of the basic building blocks for all things—neutrons, protons, electrons, quarks. Physicist Paul Davies calls the rational pattern binding all things together "the Mind of God."

This order continually flirts with disorder. Then, out of chaos, beautiful new forms emerge. The unexpected and unforeseeable happens. What we have is a self-organizing universe. It is filled with processes that start without any outside influence, and proceed in chaotic, unpredictable ways. The formation of stars is a good example. A star begins as a gaseous cloud. Eventually the universe transforms itself from random gas clouds into billions of galaxies. Star formation is driven forward by its own gravitational energy. Even after their initial formation, stars continue to develop. They burn their hydrogen and collapse, forming second- and third-generation stars that are ever more complex.

Like a choreographer who introduces bold new dances, the universe continually presents us with original works. This applies especially to the appearance of life and mind. In *Vital Dust*, the Nobel Prize-winning biologist Christian de Duve discusses the origin and evolution of life. The universe is about fifteen billion years old. But de Duve believes the primeval dust itself carried with it the potential, perhaps even the certainty, of achieving life. There is a life force, which de Duve calls a cosmic imperative, deeply imbedded in Creation. From the very beginning, our universe was precisely prepared for the emergence of life and consciousness. Humans appeared against enormous odds and by a series of coincidences of great improbability. The tiniest variation in things would have made life and mind impossible.

Does this degree of accuracy in the conditions necessary for the emergence of life point to a Creator? De Duve prefers to stay out of that heated debate and remain within what he considers to be the confines of science. But he does believe the evidence shows that life and mind are not accidents, but are woven into the fabric of the universe from the beginning. He is convinced that the universe is not an absurd joke; it has direction and meaning. It was made to give birth to thinking beings who could know

96

truth and appreciate beauty, suffer evil and yearn for goodness, feel love and experience mystery. De Duve does not use the name *God* for the source of this meaning, because he sees it as a term loaded with too many interpretations. Rather, he lays out his scientific picture and lets readers draw their own conclusions.

Dante's Rose of Fire

Meditation on the cosmos takes us again to Dante's *Paradiso*. His poem about paradise is about the universe as God's art, about physical reality as God's self-expression. For Dante, to see the universe truly was to know God. At one point in the *Paradiso*, he asks the reader to look away from his lines of poetry to the source of their message, the word spoken in the universe's wonders. Seen in relation to this transcendent Mystery, every bit of creation has lasting significance.

In Dante's *Divine Comedy*, the divine is named not only as light, but also as fire. Its culminating metaphor is an immense white rose created by the divine light as it reflects off the highest sphere of the material world. It is the Rose of Paradise, in which we encounter the deepest mystery of all loves.

And if the lowest rank encloses within itself
so great a light, how vast is the spread
of this rose in its outermost leaves!
(30.115–117)

This cosmic rose has distinct petals, composed of persons eternally alive, their individual experiences transformed by increasing insight and love. The model for Dante's experience in the heavens is rooted in St. Paul: "For now we see in a mirror dimly, but then we will see face to face. Now I know only in part; then I will know fully, even as I have been fully known" (1 Cor 13:12). Dante's final canto describes all things as bound together by the motion of divine Love, which every natural thing in the universe reflects.

FOR PRAYER AND REFLECTION

Celtic Blessings

The songs, poems, prayers, and blessings handed down from generation to generation by Celtic Christians are meant for all the seasons of life from birth to death. They come from a people who lived close to the earth, aware of the forces of nature. The following blessings are a way of entering together into a moment of praise and gratitude. In offering these blessings to another, we seek for them the well-being that accompanies reverence for the gifts of the cosmos.

> The goodness of storm be thine,
> The goodness of moon be thine,
> The goodness of sun be thine.
>
> The goodness of sea be thine,
> The goodness of earth be thine,
> The goodness of heaven be thine.
>
> The grace of the love of the skies be thine,
> The grace of the love of the stars be thine,
> The grace of the love of the moon be thine,
> The grace of the love of the sun be thine.

12. The Mystery in Our Midst

*Love is the voice of eternity
in our heart.*
　　—Elizabeth Johnson

ngels populate the heaven of artists such as Michelangelo and Handel. In the pages of the Bible, where they appear often, angels are messengers connecting us with the divine. They link heaven and Earth, making God's presence known. Recently angels have received more attention on Earth, showing up in books, cards, and conversations. A father declares at the funeral of his young son that there is now a new angel in heaven. A mother whose daughter perished in the World Trade Center tells about receiving reassurance from an angel on the night of the attack. The light that always shone through a hall window was especially bright that night, and for a moment there was a smiling angel in the light, letting her know that her daughter was all right.

Several decades ago, the sociologist Peter Berger wrote a small volume in which he points to the mystery that is all around us but easy to miss. Berger titles his book *A Rumor of Angels* because he thinks there is something to be said for these beings of light that witness to the divine presence. Stories of angels assure us that God is actively present to our lives. The traditional belief that even the most insignificant person has their own guardian angel tells us that no one lies outside the scope of this concern.

These hints of something more in our daily reality, which Berger calls "signals of transcendence," also link what is already happening now with what we hope for after death. There are many traces of eternity in our midst, glimpses of the God living deep within and around us. In the previous chapter we looked at some of those found in nature. Here the focus is on human life. For his signals of transcendence, or "rumors of angels," Berger selects order, play, hope, justice, and humor. My own list keeps humor and hope, but adds beauty, forgiveness, and love.

Humor

After my brother-in-law was diagnosed with incurable colon cancer, I marveled at his continuing capacity for deep laughter. It was not denial. He clearly grasped his condition. Yet laughter welled up from within him. He confessed that he expected the chemotherapy clinic to be grim and somber. What a surprise, he said, to find the other cancer patients sharing jokes and stories. Seven of the patients no longer had any hair. One had been up all night vomiting. They had lost many things, but not their sense of humor.

Nor had the actress and comedienne Gilda Radner, who died of ovarian cancer in 1989. The TV movie *Gilda Radner: It's Always Something* describes how a key moment came for Radner at a cancer support group called The Wellness Community. It was there that Gilda discovered how her humor could help those who had cancer, and also bring her a joy she was missing. She comments to her husband, Gene Wilder, "I'm telling ya, Gene, cancer needs me. It's got a bad reputation. It needs me to come in there and liven it up."

Humor breaks the frame, attesting to something that transcends present limits. It is a glimmer of redemption. For a moment we burst out of life's boundaries. With laughter we become survivors, even though we are still caught. We anticipate something. Not entirely bound by suffering and pain, we laugh

100

at the incongruity of our present state of affairs. The situation is not final. It cannot confine the spirit.

Beauty

In Peter Schaffer's play *Amadeus*, the aged composer Salieri comments on Mozart's music. He finds it expressive of such unfulfillable longing that "it seemed to me that I had heard a voice of God." When Salieri gazes at the original score for Mozart's Twenty-ninth Symphony, he realizes that he is "staring through the cage of those meticulous ink strokes at—an Absolute Beauty." In all the elements that make for beauty in any medium—loveliness, order, form—we sense and respond to something of the Beyond. Music is one of the clearest examples of this. It takes us into the depths.

"Ultimate Beauty" is one classic way of naming the divine. The experience of beauty both gives us a taste of what we most deeply long for, and hungers beyond our limited having of it. In *Doctor Zhivago*, Boris Pasternak says of his heroine, Lara:

> Lara was not religious. She did not believe in ritual. But sometimes, to be able to bear life, she needed the accompaniment of an inner music. She could not always compose such a music for herself. That music was God's word of life, and it was to weep over it that she went to church.

Art is not all sweetness. It does not flinch from the ugly, painful, and evil. Hearing music we somehow know in the same moment that the Mystery is both here and not here.

Artists of all kinds introduce us to the depth of the human. Unless it is clad in flesh and blood, the eye cannot see it. In their paintings, songs, and sculptures, artists bring order and unity to disparate elements. They hold the world still long enough for us to glimpse its beauty. The painter Vincent Van Gogh shows us the quiet dignity and strength of peasants in their fields. The interior of a Gothic cathedral opens into communion with infinite horizons, revealing in a structure of stone our reach toward the sacred. Beauty in all its forms transports us to new worlds.

Forgiveness

Genuine forgiveness may be one of the hardest things for an individual or a community to extend. That is why it is often considered a gift of God, not a human achievement. Human attempts at forgiveness are blocked by self-defense and the desire for revenge. Rage rises from the suffering we experience. We are so keenly aware of the faults of others, so blind to our own. Forgiveness, whether offered to others or received from them, finally feels like grace.

A woman describes such an experience. For decades she carried the pain caused by classmates who ridiculed and rejected her during grade school and high school. Then on the first day of a weekend retreat, she was alone on a bench. Suddenly she found herself able to forgive these hurts. "My first thought," she recalled, "was to wonder where in the world this peace came from? I knew God was part of it. I had tried and tried to get past this resentment, and now I could finally let go of it."

Jesus tries to keep us attentive to these openings. He points to the salvation that is already occurring, the redemption that we are too blind to see. He asks us to notice how ordinary events reveal the divine: fathers welcoming home deadbeat sons, people losing things and then being surprised by joy. And he tells us that these experiences hold promise of a fullness still to come.

We start on our way to heaven when we learn to forgive, or accept the forgiveness of others. This is clear in the Orthodox Church's celebration of the Pascha:

This is the day of resurrection.
Let us be illumined by the feast.
Let us embrace each other.
Let us call "Brothers" even those that hate us,
And forgive all by the resurrection.

102

Forgiveness breaks the cycle of human violence, bringing Easter straight into ordinary life. No wonder it is one of the first gifts the Risen Jesus offers the disciples who abandoned him in his darkest hour: "Peace be with you."

Hope

Centuries of horror, tragedy, and pain have not been able to extinguish the human capacity for hope. Hope testifies to the holiness within human beings, and to the possibility of a reality greater than death and destruction in all their forms. It is especially moving when it occurs in the face of terrible suffering and death. A horrific tale from Central America's civil war gives stark expression to the courage born from such hope. The poet Joy Harjo tells the story.

There was a massacre in El Salvador. The soldiers had gathered all the men and boys in the church at the center of the town and killed them. Then the women and girls were taken to the fields and raped and killed. One particularly beautiful one was assaulted by many soldiers before they left her to die. She began her song as she was pushed down into the dirt and did not stop singing, no matter what they did to her. She sang of the dusky mountains who watched them that day from the clouds. She sang of the love of a boy and a girl. She sang of flowers and the aroma of the moon as it linked the night with dawn. She did not stop singing. She is still singing. Can you hear her?

Such courage can only be grounded in a hope that defies death itself. In spite of all the reasons to despair, the human heart clings to hope.

Listening to people's stories through the years as a therapist, I have been struck many times not only by how very difficult life is for many people, but by how resilient human beings are. They bear, with grace and optimism, chronic diseases like major depression, Parkinson's, and stroke. They learn to walk and talk again after illness and accidents. They watch their businesses fail, and start over. That such hope exists at all, when there are so many forces to choke it, is a marvel. A woman living with multiple sclerosis talks about it: "I don't know where the strength to keep on trying has come from. But it's not something I thought I could do. That doesn't mean I have a close personal relationship with God. Often there is just a void. But I think my ability to hope—I'm convinced that's been grace."

Hope reaches toward what is not yet a reality, but could be. Despair, by contrast, traps us in the present, blinding us to alternatives. The core of hope is the expectation that the future will bring what is needed to redeem the present. Hopelessness, on the other hand, is the inability to imagine that there is any possibility of help.

We sustain hope in one another. It lives in community. It is the helping hand that grasps our own when we feel we cannot go on. Hope is charged with intimations of eternity. It is one of those signs that there must be something more than we can name, quietly at work.

Love

A mother recently told me the story of her daughter's struggle to live with bipolar disorder. The daughter had been on and off medications several times, and began to doubt that she could ever really make it in life. Then a friend came into her life, a young man who knew something about her disease and loved her in the midst of its chaos and pain. "He's an angel," the mother said. "That's what I think an angel is—someone who helps you believe that grace is real."

Surveys show that many people believe in life after death precisely because they have known love. Love lives the language of *forever*. We are reluctant to end a wonderful visit and put a dear friend on a plane bound for home. We drink in the uplifted face of a grandchild and long to live to see her bloom. Gabriel Marcel said it eloquently, and has been quoted ever since. To say that we really love someone is instinctively to insist: "Thou, at least, thou shalt not die." My husband has turned this into a line he often puts at the end of a birthday greeting for cherished family and friends: "May you live forever."

Love pushes toward union. The biblical Song of Songs, the Book of Revelation, and the poetry of mystics all use the imagery of sexual love to symbolize our relationship with God. Human love both fulfills our desire for intimacy, and awakens the yearning for a love that cannot be realized in this life. We find in the first epistle of John a description of love's power to be a foretaste of the final meeting with God:

Whoever does not love does not know
God, for God is love…

No one has ever seen God;
if we love one another,
God lives in us,
and his love is perfected in us. (1 John 4:8, 12)

Here in Washington we live in the shadow of Mount Rainier. Days go by when the mountain is shrouded in cloud cover, invisible to natives and tourists alike. Then the clouds part, and we say that the mountain is out. Once again it stands there in its breathtaking splendor. Of course, it has been there all the time, just hidden from view. In the same way, human life is filled with moments of transcendent grace. These are hints of the Holy, rumors of angels, harbingers of what is to come.

FOR PRAYER AND REFLECTION

This Celtic prayer becomes a meditation on the way God's strength and care encompass us from life to death.

God to enfold me,
God to surround me,
God in my speaking,
God in my thinking.

God in my sleeping,
God in my waking,
God in my watching,
God in my hoping.

God in my life,
God in my lips,
God in my soul,
God in my heart.

God in my sufficing,
God in my slumber,
God in mine ever-living soul,
God in mine eternity.

Rumors of Angels: A Meditation

Return in memory to a time when you experienced beauty, forgiveness, hope, or some other glimpse of Transcendence.

Relive the experience in detail and let its power again grace you. Give thanks for it. ·

—Kathleen Fischer

13. Second Chances

If you are here unfaithfully with us,
you're causing terrible damage.
If you've opened your loving to God's love,
you're helping people you don't know
and have never seen.

—Rumi

ecently a friend sorted through old boxes as she prepared to move to a new house. Timeworn letters and pictures evoked remorse for opportunities missed: "What was I thinking? I saw my stupidity. I felt sinful and sad." I often hear similar laments. So much is broken that we cannot mend. Some wounds never heal. Certain losses cannot be recouped. "Life is so imperfect," a client says. "We're just muddling through." A husband dying of lung cancer tells his wife how he regrets that he did not tell her more often how much he loved her. Then there is the wrenching sorrow that comes with hearing a dying loved one conclude: "I wasted my life."

Most of us die suspended somewhere between seriously sinful and clearly saved, like a trapeze artist who never falls to his death, but cannot quite soar either. Along with the realization of how imperfectly we have lived comes a widespread sense that it is not quite fair to have only one chance at it. Life is complex and difficult to negotiate. Generational sins shadow us. We revisit the same struggles repeatedly, our best efforts to prevail proving fruitless. In short, even if we live to a ripe old age, death does not find us proficient at loving. Two different beliefs—reincarnation and purgatory—envision a second opportunity to get it right. Another belief, that there is a hell, attests to the possibility that we could fail forever.

Reincarnation

Walking beside the Ganges River in India some years ago, it struck me how all encompassing the Hindu view of life and death is. The pilgrims who surround the funeral pyres on the riverbank take for granted that each person is being continually reborn. Birth and death are not beginning and end, but simply markers on a long journey. This belief in the protracted pilgrimage of the soul offers solutions to many intractable religious questions. It fits with the way things pass away and return in new forms. It puts less focus on each individual, and attends more to the community of all beings. It logically follows that we must do no harm to any living thing. Reincarnation also provides assurance that some part of us is immortal, yet bears the imprint of our deeds and attachments. Thus we reap what we sow, though it may not be evident in this life. This not only satisfies the human thirst for justice; it also makes sense of life's many sufferings

Though the term is used at times loosely as a synonym for the immortality of the soul, reincarnation in its classical Hindu form is actually a difficult state of human bondage. A person is continually being reborn, each rebirth a mere marker rather than an ending. What a person does or thinks in each life shapes the condition, circumstances, and impulses of future lives, just as the dispositions of this life result from past actions.

Buddhism adopted this general Hindu view of *samsara*, the endless cycle of death and rebirth, but merged and modified it with its own teachings. One thing the Eastern sages agreed on: They did not rest easily with the continual cycle of death and rebirth. Dying once is difficult; dying again and again is wearisome. So in Eastern religions the question arose: Is there no way out of this endless cycle of birth, death, and rebirth? Hindu,

Buddhist, Jainist, and Sikh answers differ, but each involves some kind of release, enlightenment, or awakening. The ultimate goal of Hinduism is *moksha*, the Sanskrit term for freedom, which can be experienced even in this life when one realizes the identity of Atman with Brahman, that is, of self with the Ultimate. Buddhist enlightenment can likewise be found in this life, when the ego is liberated from its illusions. But the ultimate hope is that beyond physical death as well, the cycle of birth and death will end, giving way to final transformation.

Belief in reincarnation is widely accepted, not only among Hindus and Buddhists, but also by those of other faiths. The Jewish kabbalistic mysticism of the Middle Ages taught that souls pre-exist, descend into matter, and then return to their divine source through a long series of reincarnations. After dying out for decades, this Jewish mystical tradition is now seeing a revival. In the forms of reincarnation most popular in the West, there is less emphasis on the doctrine of karma, and greater stress on how rebirth holds the promise of many lifetimes. This provides consolation and hope for ongoing growth. The fact that we live more than once on this Earth allows us to correct our mistakes and get better each time around.

Purgatory

Another approach to finding release from the past is called purgatory. My immediate association with purgatory is how determined I was, growing up Catholic, to chalk up as many indulgences as possible. This zealous period was not the high point of my religious development. If gaining the indulgence required visiting a church, I was in and out again many times at breakneck speed. Of course I applied some of these indulgences to saving the "poor souls in purgatory"; but most were intended for my own salvation.

Purgatory is a Catholic teaching unfamiliar to most Protestants and those without church connections. But prior to the Protestant Reformation in the sixteenth century, belief in purgatory was nearly universal among Christians. It developed from the realization that at death many of us are not quite ready to meet God, yet not so sinful that we deserve hell either. It also grew out of the Jewish and Christian practice of remembering the dead in prayer. Purgatory was a process of purification after death before entrance into paradise. By praying for the dead, we could shorten their time of purification. However, purgatory's association with indulgences, and all the serious abuses they entailed, led to its rejection by the Reformers. Protestant views of the afterlife subsequently included only heaven and hell. Even among Catholics, purgatory has gradually dropped from view.

In its current retrieval, purgatory is seen not so much as an experience of painful purgation, but as a transforming encounter with divine Love. G. K. Chesterton once made a trenchant observation about the story of "Beauty and the Beast": A thing must be loved before it is lovable. It is not that we are beautiful and therefore loved. No, we become beautiful because we are loved. Freed from its historical abuses, this renewed notion of purgatory expresses hope for a purification that begins in this life and is completed at death.

In her novel *Their Eyes Were Watching God*, Zora Neale Hurston supplies a helpful image for this grace that frees the potential concealed within us. The novel's main character, Janie, is struggling with hatred for her grandmother. Though God made us "out of stuff that sung all the time and glittered all over," Janie now sees that "most humans didn't love one another nohow." She believes that the jewel inside us has been beaten down until it has become only small sparks, albeit sparks that can still shine and sing. Then even these are covered over by mud. Purification washes away this caked mud so that the jewel of Creation can shine with its intended brilliance. Purgation is not only about what we have been; it includes the promise of what we might become.

Our purgatory, both now and in death, is shaped by the ways we hide from the light, the barriers we erect against the love bonding all beings. Though its purpose is not punishment, purgatory may include judgment. Those who survive near-death experiences — along with others who have faced life-threatening events — commonly report a life review. In an instant their whole life passes before them. Anyone who has ever tried to look unblinkingly at who they are and what they have done knows the pain of such judgment. What we call the final judgment might be understood, then, not as some external pronouncement, but as our conscience, illumined by God's light, judging our own lives.

Though this naked self-knowledge is exacting, it is ultimately redeeming. Perhaps C. S. Lewis was not far from the mark when, in acknowledging that he was probably a much more annoying person than he knew, he wondered whether in purgatory we would see our faces and hear our voices as they really are. It is only in the presence of a larger mercy that we can bear to acknowledge both the darkness and the dawn in our stories.

Belief in a purifying process like purgatory addresses another perplexing issue. What about those we do not want to see in the next life? There are people we dislike. Some have inflicted emotional or physical pain from which we have never healed. Like heaven and hell, purgatory must be a relational process, a healing of relationships more complete than anything previously experienced. Those we do not want to meet in heaven are, along with us, purified in a full encounter with divine love. The transformation paves the way for levels of reconciliation not possible in this life.

Hell

Like purgatory, hell begins here. Ask anyone who has watched a loved one being tortured in one of the many genocides that have ravaged human history, seen a friend die of a disfiguring disease like AIDS, or stood helpless as a spouse was led to the gas chambers at Auschwitz. In *The Fate of the Earth*, Jonathan Schell adds to this list the likely scenario after a full-scale nuclear explosion. The existence of these hells is too tangible to question. The hell we wonder about is the one traditionally included among the last things. Does it exist? How could a loving God damn someone to everlasting torment? And yet how could anything short of eternal damnation for some be a fitting recompense for evils beyond description in human history?

The issue of hell has been further complicated by its use through the centuries as a political and religious weapon. Rather than resolving the problem of evil, this utilization of hell has created its own form of it. The threat of eternal damnation was invoked to make "heretics" renounce their beliefs. It was used, with reinforcement from the sword, to make converts to the faith, with little sense of what they were embracing. The power to damn someone to hell reinforced religious authority, and became an instrument of terrible oppression. Beginning with the early Hebrews' denunciation of their enemies, human beings have summoned God as judge to punish those they hate. Artists painted their enemies into appropriate layers of hell, and common speech has turned to hell for the language of impotent rage. A man recently confronted the murderer of his son during a court sentencing: "I hope you burn in hell forever."

In the popular imagination, hell evokes pictures of a descent into a blazing abyss. Jesus' parables of the worthy and unworthy servants, and the sheep and the goats, provide one source for these images (Matt 25:14–46). But these metaphors are not meant to be taken literally, a point that seems easier to grasp with the sheep and goats than with the eternal fire and gnashing of teeth. Jesus does preach a future retribution for present deeds of inhumanity and injustice. But it is not clear that he is referring to an everlasting punishment. Some scholars find strong arguments against it, since eternal condemnation could never lead to the restoration of the sinner. Nor is it in keeping with the unlimited Love of God, the very heart of the good news.

A certain consensus is emerging regarding hell, though it leaves some dilemmas unresolved. It is difficult to imagine that

112

a merciful God would allow someone to be lost forever. But there is reluctance to abandon entirely the notion of hell, which testifies to the reality of human freedom and the possibility that a person can completely turn against God and others. Those in hell are there by choice; they have locked the windows and doors that might let in the light. John's Gospel conveys this sense of judgment as something we impose on ourselves when we fail to recognize Divine Reality: "And this is the judgment, that light has come into the world, and people loved darkness rather than light because their deeds were evil" (3:19).

What we know of the circumstances that limit human freedom—genetic inheritance, childhood trauma and abuse, physical and emotional illness, poverty, and racism—leaves us wondering if anyone is entirely free when locking those doors. It is also increasingly difficult to see how, given the intrinsic relatedness of all Creation, there could be a New Creation when some beings are frozen forever in torment. This leads many to question at least the everlasting nature of hell.

As for what constitutes hell, it is no longer commonly seen as a place, but as a state one works oneself into, a state of absolute isolation. One man I saw in therapy described his present existence that way. He felt like an atom adrift in the universe. In *Till We Have Faces*, C. S. Lewis suggests that the way to avoid the experience of heaven is to stay "hard at work, to hear no music, never to look at earth or sky, and (above all) to love no one." The movement of evil has always been toward nonbeing. In this century, as in previous eras, it has produced countless body bags, millions of displaced persons, and burning cities. In a universe in which everything is intrinsically related, choosing consistently and finally to hate, and in doing so, to break all ties with others, may mean nonexistence. Crimes of hatred require that we see other beings as worthless. If such exclusion of others completely narrows the circle that sustains us, we would finally cease to be. Whether anyone actually ends up in this kind of hell, or whether it lasts forever, are questions still subject to debate.

113

It may seem that in considering life after death, we have allotted too much space to heaven and too little to hell. Some believe that reviving hell's vigor would have a salutary impact on our social life. Certainly many preachers have used hellfire as the jumping off point for calls to conversion. But as tempting as that approach may seem, it does not mirror biblical and theological emphases. The larger reality has always been the all-encompassing Love of God and the divine desire for the redemption of all Creation. If the Hebrew and Christian Scriptures tell us anything, it is that God gives us all every possible chance to embrace one another in love rather than back ourselves forever into a corner of hate.

FOR PRAYER AND REFLECTION

Psalm 1

Blessed are those
who walk hand in hand
with goodness,
who stand beside virtue,
who sit in the seat of truth;
For their delight is in the Spirit of Love,
and in Love's heart they dwell
day and night.
They are like trees planted by
streams of water,
that yield fruit in due season,
and their leaves flourish;
And in all that they do, they give life.
The unloving are not so;
they are like dandelions which
the wind blows away.
Turning from the Heart of Love
they will know suffering and pain.

They will be isolated from wisdom;
for Love knows the way of truth,
the way of ignorance will perish.

—Nan Merrill

A Ritual of Atonement

Find a simple way to undo something harmful you have done.
Ask forgiveness. Write a letter of reconciliation. Plant a tree.
Tend a garden. Volunteer for a good cause. Help someone who
is ill. Use talents you have neglected.

—Kathleen Fischer

14. Justice and Mercy

Surely goodness and mercy will follow me
all the days of my life,
and I will live in God's radiance
forever and ever.

—Psalm 23

n ancient Buddhist tale tells of an encounter between the Buddha and a woman who has lost her only child. Deeply distraught, she comes to the Buddha, convinced that he has the power to bring her child back to life. The Buddha agrees to fulfill her request if she can bring him a seed from a household in her village that has not known pain. So the woman knocks on door after door, only to hear one story after another of sorrow. She returns to tell the Buddha that all have endured suffering.

Not only is suffering universal, it is unevenly distributed. As Afghanistan starts to rebuild after twenty years of brutal war, major earthquakes rock it. The majority of those killed by the tremors, and many killed in the wars, are children. Closer to home, death prematurely cuts down family and friends. Unspeakable crimes of torture, rape, and murder go unpunished. Add to this global hunger, slavery, and natural disasters. No wonder we yearn for justice and mercy.

Justice

The scope of injustice in the world is one of the strongest arguments for heaven and hell. The Bible assures us from early on that the good will be rewarded and the evil punished. But it seems so rarely to happen here. In fact, evil often prospers. What are we to think? Does the universe operate in a completely random fashion? Or is there a just God who is present to it? The Hebrew Bible's oldest undisputed reference to the resurrection of the dead proposes an answer that echoes down through the centuries. We find it in the Book of Daniel.

Many of those who sleep in the dust of the earth shall awake, some to everlasting life, and some to shame and everlasting contempt. Those who are wise shall shine like the brightness of the sky, and those who lead many to righteousness, like the stars forever and ever. (12:2–3)

Our actions do indeed have consequences, not only for this life, but also in the life to come. This gives the highest moral seriousness to what we do.

The Hebrew Scriptures contain another early expression of belief in an afterlife. It provides a reason to hope when facing injustice. The verse occurs in the story of a mother who watches her seven sons tortured and killed before her eyes. It is the middle of the second century BCE. The brothers die because they have defied the Greek tyrant Antiochus Epiphanes and remained faithful to their own religious traditions. It is perplexing to their faith that this act of bravery is not rewarded here and now.

But the martyrdom account of the seven Maccabean brothers declares quite directly that God will rescue them from eternal death. Their mother compares God's vindication of her children to her own creative experience of giving them birth.

Therefore the Creator of the world, who shaped the beginning of humankind and devised the origin of all things, will

in his mercy give life and breath back to you again. (2
Macc 7:23)

The grief-stricken mother's words evoke the fertile waters of
Genesis. She declares that even in death we are held in a loving
womb from which new being arises. Evil does not have the last
word. God can resurrect her sons from dust, or even from nothing, if necessary.

Although they provide a foundation for future hope, biblical
writings also make clear that we cannot simply sit back and wait
for God to make everything right in the end. The writings of the
Hebrew prophets, which provide the imagery for many depictions
of both present and future hope, focus on renewal of the entire
Creation in this present life. They cry out against present injustice,
and call for repentance now. They threaten disastrous consequences if the present course continues. The *shalom* or peace they
describe is not something that will come to pass in another place
and time. It is meant to happen here, and soon. It anticipates a
long and full life in the shade of one's own vine and in community. Nature will be healed, and the lion will lie down with the
lamb. Old age and youth will both be valued. The new heaven
and Earth are meant to be realized in the cosmos we know.

But hope for divine justice does not support revenge scenarios. Its goal is not to destroy, but to redeem and save. It is a
restorative judgment, not a divine version of our throw-it-away
culture. Divine anger is brief; divine Love is lifelong. The Bible
employs down-home images to suggest this: a refiner's fire that
removes dross and alloy, a dirty dish that is washed clean for
reuse. In talking about the judgment day, for example, the
prophet Isaiah balances several elements: danger and death, but
also homecoming celebrations and delicious dinners. There are
earthshaking events, but also an end to tears and mourning. This
is the kind of restorative justice sought in situations such as
South Africa's healing from apartheid, where the goal is to con-
front evil in a way that permits life to go on and people to live in
peace with one another.

Hope for this kind of justice surfaces in a local story of injury and pain. In March of last year, a pastor was training for the Seattle-to-Portland bicycle race, which he intended to do with his daughter. A car with two teenagers in it pulled alongside him as he rode. Startled, he glanced over at them, then turned his head back to the road. Just then, a seventeen-year-old boy leaned out the passenger window of the car and pushed him. The pastor crashed, as he heard laughter coming from the car. Months later he is still in severe pain from the injuries to his elbow, shoulder, ribs, and lung. He can no longer type or lift things the way he once could. The most haunting thing of all for him is the memory of the laughter. Yet he has begun a weekly series at his church on the topic of forgiveness. He wants prosecutors to find a creative kind of justice, perhaps by having the teenagers work with accident victims or with people trying to rehabilitate from injuries. He is searching for the kind of restorative justice we hope for in life beyond death, the kind that allows us to reconcile, heal, and make a fresh beginning.

Justice is larger than judgment. While it may initially be satisfying to call down God's wrath on our enemies, our lives are yoked with theirs, and often we, too, are at fault. That is why the Gospel describes salvation as reconciliation. It has an essentially social and cosmic dimension.

Mercy

As adults we come to realize that the world does not divide neatly into good and bad people. Each of us is at times cruel and vengeful, unconcerned and unforgiving. And each of us is at times generous and loving. I remember early in my work as a therapist when I was seeing clients who struggled with hatred, murderous thoughts, violence, and revenge. My supervisor asked me if I recognized these same tendencies in myself. When I said, "Yes," she replied, "Good, then you will understand them in others." There is not one of us who does not need mercy. And the

119

sobering Gospel message is that "the measure you give will be the measure you get back" (Luke 6:38). To choose mercy for others is at the same time to hope for it for ourselves.

Among the ninety-nine names for Allah in the Qur'an are Mercy, Forbearance, Generosity, Love, and Compassion. The parables of Jesus affirm the justice of God. But they speak even more of God's mercy. The good are separated from the evil in Matthew's parables of the worthy and unworthy servants, and of the sheep and the goats. What we do now has consequences for the world to come. But the attitude of God is also portrayed as that of the father of the prodigal son—a welcoming, forgiving embrace of the sinful but lovable human being.

The poet Jane Kenyon describes beautifully in "Notes from the Other Side" how trust in divine mercy sustains our visions of life beyond death. She speaks of letting go of despair and fear, of illness and poverty. In her vision of the afterlife there are no credit cards or insurance premiums; there is no more death. Her poem concludes:

and God, as promised, proves
to be mercy clothed in light.

Mercy is the discretion a judge has to pardon. It is the compassion shown an offender, the kindly forbearance we had no right to expect.

There is one meditation on the meaning of mercy that engages me particularly. It comes from a person who lived in a small cottage in fourteenth-century England, a woman who has become known as Julian of Norwich. When she was about thirty years old, Julian had a series of visions that came to her during an illness in which she thought she was dying. She wrote a brief account of these revelations shortly after they occurred, and then thought about them for twenty years before composing further reflections.

To appreciate this mystic's insights, it is important to take note of her historical circumstances. She lived in a time of terror and tragedy. The Hundred Years War was raging. The Black Death had struck Norwich in 1349, killing a third of its people. A severe famine occurred in 1369 and peasant revolts followed in its wake. Violence and chaos were everywhere. The church was drowning in corruption and the blind pursuit of power, which included, in 1377, the scandal of two rival popes. Guilt and fear of eternal punishment grew as the darkness of the age deepened.

When Julian states her now famous conviction that "all will be well," it is no facile optimism. In the midst of a culture bent on revenge, she drafts a fresh understanding of redemption, based not on God's wrath but on divine mercy. For a moment, she says, she sees the world as God sees it. God looks on us with compassion, not blame. He could not hate what he has created. By speaking of this divine Love as *homely*, a Middle English word that sounds a bit quaint to us, Julian emphasizes the closeness of God's Love. The *homely* is the intimate, the familiar. She uses a variety of images to bring home this tender love: God is our natural place, created by a motherhood of love; the womb that encloses us; the clothing that wraps and shelters us. We are God's home.

This Love of God is not just for human beings, but for all Creation. Julian is shown something small, no bigger than a hazelnut, lying in the palm of her hand: "I was amazed that it could last, for I thought that because of its littleness it would suddenly have fallen into nothing. And I was answered in my understanding: It lasts and always will, because God loves it; and thus everything has being through the love of God." Of Creation, she says, this is surely true: God made it, God loves it, God preserves it.

Julian is left with lots of questions: What are we to make of sin, God's anger, and divine judgment? In theorizing about redemption, she attends less to sin and more to the dimensions of divine Love. Her work is a commentary on John's statement that "God is love, and those who abide in love abide in God, and God abides in them" (1 John 4:16). What she adds to reflection on the meaning of the afterlife is the caution that human judgment is not the same as divine judgment; God is much more loving that we can grasp. Seeing how God can bring together justice and mercy may be the most remarkable of all the revelations we encounter when we die.

The End of the World

It was during Christmas week last year that I set out to read what scientists are saying about the end of the world. It was not a diversion calculated to increase my holiday cheer. The scenarios were chilling. The universe, according to predictions, is a futile enterprise that will end either in a fiery conflagration when it collapses on itself, or in cosmic decay after dissipating its energy in infinite expansion. The galaxies are being driven apart by the expanding force of the Big Bang, all the while being pulled back together by the contracting force of gravity. It is not clear which side will win.

One approach to these projections is to assert that there are huge gaps in our knowledge, so other scenarios are also possible. Life on Earth was new when it arose four billion years ago; something as unexpected could arise in the future in a nonlinear and chaotic way impossible to predict. Cosmology, which studies the origin and history of the universe as a whole, is still young. Each new answer raises enormous questions. Two astrophysicists theorize that the universe's end will spark a fresh beginning. In about one trillion years, they believe, the universe will end in a fiery cataclysm, only to give birth to a new universe. And this scenario will repeat itself in an infinite cycle.

If we take the most widely accepted scientific scenarios seriously, they underscore the fact that science cannot establish a basis for hope. Rather, the future of the created world rests with God. Instructive here are the comments of Walter Brueggemann on the prophetic words delivered to ancient Israel in the midst of her Babylonian exile. Brueggemann says that it is exactly at the zero hour, when everything lies in shambles, that hope arises. The lyrical poetry of the prophets Isaiah, Ezekiel, and Jeremiah remembers the miracles of times past and projects them into the future—new beginnings, new homes, peace and joy again in fresh scenarios. Motifs from Eden appear in the poetry of the end.

The prophetic depictions of destruction, Brueggemann reminds us, are as cataclysmic as any scientific prediction of the end. Take, for instance, Jeremiah.

I looked on the earth, and lo, it
was waste and void;
and to the heavens, and they
had no light.
I looked on the mountains, and lo,
they were quaking,
and all the hills moved to and
fro.
I looked, and lo, there was no one
at all,
and all the birds of the air had
fled. (4:23–25)

When we hope in such times, there can be only one basis for it, the God who "calls into existence the things that do not exist" (Rom 4:17). These ancient seers not only envisage homecoming during exile, but describe a new heaven and a new Earth arising out of a crushed Creation. The creator of heaven and Earth will, by means we cannot fathom, restore all things to order, joy, and peace (Isa 65:17–25).

What of the Second Coming of Jesus? From the beginning of Christianity, his return has been associated with the end of the world. Scholars disagree as to whether the expectation of an imminent return goes back to Jesus himself. But a central aspect of Jesus' teaching certainly is his message of God's present and coming reign. Although Jesus sometimes speaks of the future coming of God, he makes clear that the reign of God can be experienced even now.

123

Jesus borrows some of his language for God's future reign from the apocalyptic literature of his time. Its imagery occurs not only in his Gospel discourses (Mark 13, Matthew 24, and Luke 21), but also in the Book of Revelation. Apocalyptic passages depict world catastrophe, the supreme struggle of the powers of evil against God, and the dreadful combat in which evil is finally defeated. The dire portents found in these writings are familiar: signs in the heavens, the moon darkening and the sun giving no light, natural disasters, wars and rumors of wars.

Apocalyptic writing flourishes when times are particularly bad and people can see no way out except through a dramatic intervention by God. Its core message is the triumph of good over evil somehow by the power of God. The language used is the language of the imagination—creative images—for there is no actual sighting of the beginning or end of history. Faced with this limit, apocalyptic writing employs the suggestive power of poetry and story to express both our fears and our hopes.

Jesus' words about the end-time, like those of the prophets before him, are intended not as an exact description of the future course of events, but rather as a vivid depiction of the calamities and miseries of every age, and the necessity and validity of an abiding trust in God. "Now when these things begin to take place, stand up and raise your heads, because your redemption is drawing near" (Luke 21:28).

FOR PRAYER AND REFLECTION

A Prayer for Forgiveness

Divine Healer,
You have promised that though our
sins be red as scarlet
you will make them white as snow.

I am in need of your mercy.

In uncountable ways
I have failed to love well,
marring the beauty and harmony
of creation.

Forgive the hurt I have inflicted,
the hardness I have harbored,
the grace I have refused.

Take my regrets and mistakes,
my failed expectations,
the hatreds and betrayals
I have revealed to no one else.

Fall like fresh rain on my parched
body and spirit.
Cleanse me and heal me.

—Kathleen Fischer

Merger Poem

And then all that has divided us will merge
And then compassion will be wedded to power
And then softness will come to a world that is harsh
and unkind
And then both men and women will be gentle
And then both women and men will be strong
And then no person will be subject to another's will
And then all will be rich and free and varied
And then the greed of some will give way to the needs
of many
And then all will share equally in the Earth's
abundance

And then all will care for the sick and the weak
and the old
And then all will nourish the young
And then all will cherish life's creatures
And then all will live in harmony with each other
and the Earth
And then everywhere will be called Eden once again.

—Judy Chicago

15. Walking With the Dying

Goodbye to the Life I used to live—
And the World I used to know—
And kiss the Hills, for me, just once—
Then—I am ready to go!
                    —Emily Dickinson

hen the doctors began to fear that my mother could not fight off the pneumonia that eventually took her life, my husband and I asked if she would like us to pray with her. She said yes. So we blessed her, reminded her of God's great love and mercy, and thanked her for everything. We recited the "Good Shepherd psalm," with its familiar and comforting cadences. Then, perhaps recalling Tom's lengthy blessings before meals over the years, she said: "That's enough."

From earliest times, people have helped one another cross the divide between life and death. Ancient Egyptians, even the poorest among them, always buried something with their dead. Sometimes it was jars of beer made from barley, their daily drink, placed in tombs to ensure the dead would not go without it. Pueblo Indians buried a handful of cornmeal under the arms of those who had led good lives. It was meant to be sustenance for their journey to the world of spirits from which all had emerged and to which they would return. They placed several handfuls of cornmeal under the arms of those who had led bad lives, because the journey would take longer. *The Tibetan Book of the*

Dead has guided those in the East who accompany others through physical death, the after-death state, and eventual rebirth. It tells how to be with a person as sadness, anger, guilt, or fear break over them, how to send thoughts of love and encouragement that free the dying from fear and false paths.

It is a great gift to help someone die well. And spiritual support is as important for the dying as physical care and pain control. A 1997 Gallup Poll asked Americans what sort of support they want in their final hours and what they worry about most. At least half of the respondents identified four things as very important: having someone with them who could share their fears and concerns, simply having someone with them, having the opportunity to pray alone, and having someone pray with them. Nearly half also said that when they thought about dying, they worried a great deal that God would not forgive them.

When ancient rituals echo and support a dying person's faith, they resonate with comfort and power. For Roman Catholics, the anointing of the sick with oil comforts the body and conveys God's forgiveness and ultimate healing. As death comes for a Muslim, the dying person's face is turned toward the Ka'ba in Mecca, the holiest sanctuary in Islam. The family then whispers the *shahadah* in his or her ear. This is the core statement of faith that there is no God but Allah and that Muhammad is God's prophet and messenger. Stories in the Hindu tradition also portray the saving power of God's name at the time of death. Hindus recite the divine names as a person is dying so that God will be the focus of attention. Along with these resources from our faith traditions, there are several general ways we can offer spiritual care to the dying.

Entering Into Their World

I am a very fast walker. Often, when hiking with someone, I find myself ahead on the trail. When I realize this, I usually stop to let my companion catch up. But my fast pace prevents us from making the hike together, enjoying a rhythm comfortable for us both. The same thing can happen when we accompany the dying. We can lead with our own agendas: the prayers or hymns we like, what we want to discuss, what we think is important. The person may want to concentrate on living fully, when we think they should be preparing to die. Or they may want to focus on dying when we want them to go on living.

In *Making Friends With Death: A Buddhist Guide to Encountering Mortality*, Judith Lief emphasizes how important it is to enter fully into the dying person's world. This is not so easy. We are afraid of death, and usually try to distance ourselves from it. Yet it is part of life, every life, even our own.

From the Buddhist tradition come two suggestions for expressing the love we have for the dying person. The first is to see the person as a human being like ourselves, with the same needs and fears. The second is to put ourselves directly and without flinching into their situation. What would I want and need?

When we move into this place of deeper connection, we free the dying person from the need to impress, please, or take care of us, allowing them to be as they truly are. We can in turn acknowledge our limitations in knowing what to do and how to be with them. We are there together as ordinary human beings. Often the dying person is too ill or weak to say or do anything. One way of then being present is to simply match our breath with the person's breath, be with them in silence, or touch them in some way to let them know that they are not alone. If we have a sense that they would want it, we can recite the prayers that a person no longer has the words to say.

Listening at Many Levels

In *Final Gifts*, two hospice nurses who have spent more than a decade working with the terminally ill share what they have learned from those at the end of this life. They draw insights from their own and their colleagues' years of experience, as well as from a study of more than two hundred dying persons. The nurses, Maggie Callanan and Patricia Kelley, coined the term "Nearing Death Awareness" for the special communication of the dying. This communication takes two forms: attempts of the dying to describe what they are experiencing, and requests for what they need for a peaceful death. Some of this communication is, of course, about physical comfort, pain, medications, and other matters. But that is not the focus of the stories in *Final Gifts*.

Callanan and Kelley find that the dying frequently glimpse another world. While giving few details, they talk with wonder of the peace and beauty of this place. Their descriptions are typically brief, rarely more than a sentence or two, and not very specific. The experience does not usually involve leaving their bodies; rather, while remaining in their bodies, they are aware of two existences. It does not matter that these patients are from every kind of religious background, and that some are agnostics or atheists.

The dying also report talking with, or sensing the presence of, people whom others cannot see. These are often persons they have known and loved—a parent, spouse, sibling, or friend— who has died before them. Sometimes they are religious figures or spiritual beings, like Jesus, the Buddha, or angels. Their descriptions are tentative and metaphorical.

It can be difficult to decipher a dying person's requests. They often have little strength to convey them. The messages may come in symbol or suggestion, and be easy to dismiss as simply the confusion that accompanies illness or the side effects of medication. But Callanan and Kelley believe that by listening with open minds and hearts we will hear what a person needs in order to die peacefully.

A common theme is the desire for reconciliation. The dying identify relationships that leave them feeling sad, guilty, or troubled. Reviewing their lives, many see incomplete tasks, broken ties, and missed opportunities. They need to offer an apology, express gratitude, be forgiven, or make peace with a supreme being. It is important to do whatever is possible to facilitate such reconciliation by arranging meetings or phone conversations with persons the dying person needs to talk with, bringing in chaplains they want to see, or praying with them for the forgiveness they desire and assuring them of it out of our own sense of God's goodness.

Callanan and Kelley confirm what I learned during my years of work in a nursing home. I once asked a woman dying of cancer how she was. "Fine," she said. "My sister just sat on the bed to talk with me for a while." The woman was ninety-two and her mind was very clear; her sister had died over a decade earlier. "I keep getting to the airport and missing the plane," another man told me repeatedly. As I listened, I learned that he was ready to die and could not figure out why God did not pick him up.

It is important to remember that each individual's experience is unique. Some of our nursing home residents died without giving any descriptions of their experience. Some struggled at the end. Others simply slipped into a coma and vanished. But there were those who tried to tell us what they saw and what they needed. We had to listen creatively, drawing on what we already knew about the person, to hear what they wanted us to know.

Helping to Bridge the Passage

Though the point may seem obvious, it helps when I keep in mind that dying is a transition. Like other life passages, it has several movements. It begins with letting go, with the loss of all that has been. What follows is often a vague in-between state, a place of uncertainty and doubt. Then there is movement into the unknown, sometimes with questions about what it will be like. At times death is so sudden and violent, or so prolonged and painful, that this passage is entirely outside our view or interventions. Even when it is possible to be with the dying person for some of these moments, the sequence is rarely neat. But it does suggest possible ways of supporting a dying person by helping them review their lives, let go, and grieve; feel supported and loved as death approaches; and imagine what the future holds.

Perhaps we hesitate most when it comes to imagining life after death. A terminally ill client of mine once said: "I wouldn't mind dying if I knew where I was going." Most of us can identify with this simple statement. A letter of Paul to the early Christians living in Ephesus invites them to freely explore what the length and breadth of divine Love might look like in its fullness (Eph 3:18). I suggested to my client that she do the same. Why should we not be free to find hope in such imagining as we die?

In every attempt to picture paradise, whether by poets like Dante or by dying relatives and friends, a similar process is at work. We bring to mind the mysteries of the universe and the happiest moments of human life. We recall times of beauty and joy, wonder and depth. Then we imagine what these experiences might be like if they broke free of every limitation. That is, in fact, what I have tried to do throughout this book.

What we envision is something like this: Suffering no longer exists. No child grows up in a slum with too little to eat. No one is fighting. No one is sick. People are sharing, despite all their diversity, and enjoying one another's company. Fear is gone. So is despair. Forgiveness and beauty, love and fullness, have taken their rightful place. Then we remind ourselves that what paradise will actually be like surpasses anything we can say. Peaceful now, we let the Mystery be Mystery, surrendering ourselves in trust to its goodness.

Frodo Baggins, the hero of Tolkien's *Ring* trilogy, shows how such picturing affects the way we face death. At the end of his adventures, he is victorious over the enemies of Middle Earth but comes away painfully wounded. Frodo knows that his wounds are mortal, that they will not be healed in this world. But he faces life and eventual death with calm and courage, with trust that he will find wholeness in the "far green country under a swift sunrise," where "the sound of singing comes over the water."

At the end of the Book of Revelation, the final book of the Bible, there is another imaginative vision (22:1–5). It is a city whose gates are always open, where it is always daylight. There is water that is free, and a river on either side of which is the tree of life. All are there for the healing of the nations.

FOR PRAYER AND REFLECTION

Sharing of Short Prayers

Those staying with a dying person can gather round and lay hands on him or her as they say these prayers or prayers they compose themselves. One person can serve as leader, saying the prayer that the others present then repeat.

Send (N._____) your love and your strength. *(Repeat)*
Lead us on the path of healing and hope. *(Repeat)*
We trust in your tender care. *(Repeat)*
Gracious Mystery, be with (N._____) now. *(Repeat)*
Bless (N. _____), whom we all love. *(Repeat)*
Thank you for (N.'s _____) life and love. *(Repeat)*

The following, or similar refrains, can be inserted among spontaneous prayers:

Stay with me, stay with me.
Held in love, held in love.
Full of mercy, full of mercy.

— Kathleen Fischer

A Farewell Blessing by the Person Dying

Soon I will be leaving you, my friends.
It is so hard to say goodbye.
But there are things I want to tell you before I go.

I take with me deep gratitude for all the ordinary and special times we have shared: the laughter, the difficult days, and the unforgettable memories.

Thank you from my heart for your love and your care, expressed in so many ways. Forgive me for all the times I have hurt or failed you, both those I know of and those you never told me.

I wish for each of you all the blessings life can bring. Keep on loving deeply, living fully, and enjoying the beauties of Creation.

Our lives will remain forever intertwined. Call on me when you are in need, or when you have good news to share. I will be with you in God's love, sending you strength, wisdom, and hope.

Above all, remember that I love you.

—Kathleen Fischer

Epilogue

t the end of a play, one of the actors sometimes returns to the stage to deliver a concluding speech, drawing the threads of the drama together or highlighting certain themes. I am often asked for a similar brief summation of what we can say about life after death. In response, I have developed the following ten statements. They may serve as a way of revisiting the fundamental convictions of this book.

1. While not universal, belief in life after death is widespread. It exists in many historical periods and cultures. Some are content with believing that there will be something rather than nothing, leaving the details to be discovered after death. Many others use analogies from this life to envision what the afterlife will be like. They draw on the most positive of life's experiences, without their flaws, and acknowledge the silence at the edges of all attempts to speak about it.

2. Conceptions of life after death have always been, and must always be, consistent with the worldview of the time. Many of the images we have inherited no longer speak to us. But this does not mean we cannot continue to believe in heaven and hell; fresh conceptions of these realities are possible.

3. The afterlife is most fundamentally about union with God as well as all beings, or in the case of hell, the loss of those crucial connections. God is not in some supernatural realm above us. Rather, the divine is right here, as the Ground, Depth, and Horizon of our present experience. Therefore heaven and hell are not places up above or down below. They also start here, and are extended.

4. We have intimations even now of what awaits us after death. These come both in the vast and intricate splendor of the universe, and in human experiences of humor, hope, beauty, forgiveness, and love. Our present spiritual experience attests to life beyond the material, and also provides a foretaste of that awareness, union with God, and oneness with the universe for whose fullness we hope.

5. Science offers both challenges and resources for the discussion of life after death. Scientific approaches that reduce all reality to the material miss important dimensions of our experience. However, other streams of science witness to both the mystery in the universe and the limits of science. They even offer fresh language for expressing traditional beliefs. For example, the worldview of quantum physics, which describes reality as an interconnected web of relationships, gives us new grounds for our experience of remembering and relating to those who have died, and for envisioning the social dimensions of the resurrected body.

6. A dualistic worldview, which sharply divides matter from spirit, is no longer an acceptable way of solving the problem of survival after death. The relationships between body and soul, this world and the next, self and others, are being rethought in ways that permit the possibility of ongoing life without devaluing bodies and the Earth. We and the world will be transformed and united with the Whole in ways we cannot fully grasp. The core resurrection message is that there is continuity, as well as discontinuity, between this life and the next.

7. Though we have conceived the afterlife primarily in terms of individual survival, both the biblical witness and the contemporary cosmic story describe fullness of life in terms of the connectedness of all beings. Our destinies are intertwined both now and forever.

8. Life beyond this world is demanded by our sense of justice and the widely varying stages of development in which persons leave this world. Belief in reincarnation is one way of addressing this problem. Another is the Bible's witness to both a realized and a future eschatology, terms used to say that the end times are already here but not yet fully actualized. Language about the Second Coming of Jesus, and the end-time it ushers in, is meant to convey the final realization of God's justice and mercy, along with the elimination of suffering and the power of evil.

9. The scientific account of the end of the world depicts the future in catastrophic terms. While the Bible, too, is rich in cataclysmic visions, Christian tradition holds to a vision of promise and fulfillment, redemption and hope. God is faithful to Creation, and the divine reassurance echoes across the centuries: "Be not afraid."

10. Our hope for what is to come sustains our ordinary lives and gives them direction. It upholds our prayer, awakens us to the marvels of the universe, deepens our compassion for all beings, connects us to past and future generations, and supports our struggle against suffering and evil in all their forms. Hope brightens the entire spiritual journey, not just its ending.

Notes and Further Reading

here are a number of excellent presentations of images used for heaven and hell throughout history. I found particularly helpful: Jeffrey Burton Russell, *A History of Heaven: The Singing Silence* (Princeton, N.J.: Princeton University Press, 1997); *The Book of Heaven: An Anthology of Writings from Ancient to Modern Times*, ed. Carol Zaleski and Philip Zaleski (New York: Oxford University Press, 2000); and Colleen McDannell and Bernard Lang, *Heaven: A History* (New Haven, Conn.: Yale University Press, 1988). Alice K. Turner, *The History of Hell* (New York: Harcourt Brace, 1993) is a lively and illustrated account of hell. Also illustrated, and broad in its scope, is Brian Innes, *Death and the Afterlife* (New York: St. Martin's Press, 1999).

A fine brief discussion of current questions from a Roman Catholic perspective is Peter C. Phan, *Responses to 101 Questions on Death and Eternal Life* (Mahwah, N.J.: Paulist, 1997). One of the most thorough accounts of Jewish positions is Simcha Paull Raphael, *Jewish Views of the Afterlife* (Northvale, N.J.: Jason Aronson, 1996).

Chapter 1: Invisible Realities

Paul Murray's "The Canticle of the Void" is in *Invisible Light: Poems About God*, ed. Diane Culbertson (New York: Columbia University Press, 2000), 25. Murray is speaking of the absence of God that is paradoxically God's presence in the world.

The story "The Song of the Bird" is in Anthony de Mello, *The Song of the Bird* (Chicago: Loyola University Press, 1983), 4.

Mary Midgley uses the aquarium analogy in *Science and Poetry* (New York: Routledge, 2001), 101–2.

Stannard's example is on p. 8 of his book *The God Experiment: Can Science Prove the Existence of God?* (Mahwah, N.J.: Hidden Spring, 2000). For Paul Davies' discussion of how quantum physics undermines materialism by changing the way we view matter, see Paul Davies and John Gribbin, *The Matter Myth: Dramatic Discoveries That Challenge Our Understanding of Physical Reality* (New York: Simon & Schuster, 1992).

The phrase from T. S. Eliot is from "The Dry Salvages" in *The Complete Poems and Plays: 1909–1950* (New York: Harcourt, Brace & World, 1952), 136.

A fine discussion of the meaning of spirituality, as well as criteria for evaluating the health of one's spiritual path, can be found in Thomas Hart, *Spiritual Quest: A Guide to the Changing Landscape* (Mahwah, N.J.: Paulist, 1999).

On p. 243 of her book *The Fire in the Equations: Science, Religion and the Search for God* (Grand Rapids, Mich.: William B. Eerdmans, 1994), Kitty Ferguson comments that religious experience is not exclusively or mainly private knowledge. It has been accumulating for a longer period of history, and from a wider sample of the population, than scientific knowledge.

Interesting approaches to the question of the spiritual from the scientific side are presented in *Science and the Spiritual Quest: New Essays by Leading Scientists*, ed. W. Mark Richardson, Robert John Russell, Philip Clayton, and Kirk Wegter-McNelly (New York: Routledge, 2002).

John Hick, *The Fifth Dimension: An Exploration of the Spiritual Realm* (Oxford: Oneworld Publications, 1999) is a readable and convincing argument for a view of reality in which the spiritual dimension plays a central role. He cites the findings of the Religious Experience Research Unit at Oxford University regarding the positive effects of religious or transcendent experiences in people's lives on pp. 112–17.

The approach I take to affirming both the transcendence and immanence of God is called panentheism, a view not to be confused with pantheism. The roots of this Greek word include *pan*, which means "everything," *en* which means "in," and *theos*, or God. Panentheism holds that God is in everything, and everything is in God (immanent), but that God is more than everything (transcendent). In pantheism, a Greek term that lacks the *en*, the universe and God are identified.

For a discussion of the relationship between care of the Earth and our notion of God, see Sallie McFague, *The Body of God: An Ecological Theology* (Minneapolis: Augsburg Fortress, 1993).

Denise Levertov, "In Whom We Live and Move and Have Our Being," and "Primary Wonder," in *Sands of the Well* (New York: New Directions, 1996), 107, 129.

The translation of Psalm 16 is from Stephen Mitchell, *A Book of Psalms: Selected & Adapted from the Hebrew* (New York: HarperCollins, 1993), 8.

Chapter 2: Soul Talk

I am grateful to my brother, Philip Fischer, for permission to use his poem.

For a helpful overview of the meaning of soul, see Nancey Murphy's essay "Human Nature: Historical, Scientific, and Religious Issues" in *Whatever Happened to the Soul? Scientific and Theological Portraits of Human Nature*, ed. Warren S. Brown, Nancey Murphy, and H. Newton Malony (Minneapolis: Fortress, 1998), 1–29. Others grapple with the issue of dualism and life after death in *Soul, Body, and Survival: Essays on the Metaphysics of Human Persons*, ed. Kevin Corcoran (Ithaca, N.Y.: Cornell University Press, 2001).

The Lewis Thomas material is from the chapter called "The Music of *This* Sphere" in his brief classic, *The Lives of a Cell* (New York: The Viking Press, 1974), 22–28. John Polkinghorne discusses resurrection and his theory of the soul as an information-bearing pattern in *The Faith of a Physicist: Reflections of a Bottom-Up Thinker* (Princeton, N.J.: Princeton University Press, 1994), 162–74; as well as in an essay in the volume he edited with Michael Welker, *The End of the World and the Ends of God: Science and Theology on Eschatology* (Harrisburg, Penn.: Trinity Press International, 2000), 29–41. I am also indebted to the work of John F. Haught, *Science and Religion: From Conflict to Conversation* (Mahwah, N.J.: Paulist, 1995), especially pp. 95–96; and his essay "Information and Cosmic Purpose" in the volume he edited, *Science and Religion in Search of Cosmic Purpose* (Washington, D.C.: Georgetown University Press, 2000), 105–20.

For a multifaceted depiction of biblical Wisdom, including her role as cosmic ordering principle, see Silvia Schroer, *Wisdom Has Built Her House: Studies on the Figure of Sophia in the Bible,* trans. Linda M. Maloney and William McDonough (Collegeville, Minn.: Liturgical Press, 2000). My own ideas on the relationship of soul-talk to biblical Wisdom were refined by reading Paul S. Nancarrow's article "Wisdom's Information: Rereading a Biblical Image in the Light of Some Contemporary Science and Speculation," *Zygon,* 32/1 (March 1997): 51–64.

Beatrice Bruteau draws out the Christian and Trinitarian implications of the new cosmic worldview in *God's Ecstasy: The Creation of a Self-Creating World* (New York: Crossroad, 1997). See also Diarmuid O'Murchu, *Evolutionary Faith: Rediscovering God in Our Great Story* (Maryknoll, N.Y.: Orbis, 2002).

The selection from the tribute to Sister Mary O'Connell is in "In Memoriam," *SNJM Network News* (Fall 2002): 11.

Antonio Damasio examines this experience of continuity amid change from another perspective in *The Feeling of What Happens: Body and Emotion in the Making of Consciousness* (Orlando, Fla.: Harcourt, 1999). He distinguishes between *core consciousness,* which provides us with a transient sense of self in the here and now, and *extended consciousness,* a much more complex and elaborate sense of self, which includes a lived past and an anticipated future.

The rabbi's story is told in Fritjof Capra and David Steindl-Rast, *Belonging to the Universe: Explorations on the Frontiers of Science & Spirituality* (San Francisco: Harper San Francisco, 1991), 139.

Alfred North Whitehead, *Process and Reality,* corrected edition, ed. David Ray Griffin and Donald W. Sherburne (New York: Macmillan, 1978), 346.

Elizabeth A. Johnson explores the implications of different images for God in *She Who Is: The Mystery of God in Feminist Theological Discourse* (New York: Crossroad, 1992). See also Marcus J. Borg, *The God We Never Knew: Beyond Dogmatic Religion to a More Authentic Contemporary Faith* (San Francisco: Harper San Francisco, 1997); and

Richard Elliott Friedman, *The Hidden Face of God* (San Francisco: Harper San Francisco, 1995).

Chapter 3: Metamorphosis

Nikos Kazantzakis, *The Greek Passion*, trans. Jonathan Griffin (New York: Simon & Schuster, 1953), 169.

The experience of Elisabeth Kübler-Ross at Maidanek is related in Derek Gill, *Quest: The Life of Elisabeth Kübler-Ross* (New York: Ballantine, 1980), 131.

Scientist and poet Chet Raymo taught me about the life of the butterfly and other marvels of nature in *Natural Prayers* (St. Paul, Minn.: Hungry Mind Press, 1999).

The astrophysicist Arnold Benz describes the cycle of death/resurrection found in small as well as great things in nature as the pattern of present and future hope. See his *The Future of the Universe: Chance, Chaos, God?* (New York: Continuum, 2000.)

Sandra M. Schneiders brings Jesus' meeting with Mary Magdalene to life in *Written That You May Believe: Encountering Jesus in the Fourth Gospel* (New York: Crossroad, 1999), 189–201. My thinking on the meaning of the resurrection has also been shaped by the essays in *The Resurrection: An Interdisciplinary Symposium on the Resurrection of Jesus*, ed. Stephen T. Davis, Daniel Kendall, and Gerald O'Collins (New York: Oxford University Press, 1997); and Pheme Perkins, *Resurrection: New Testament Witness and Contemporary Reflection* (New York: Doubleday, 1984).

I have learned a great deal about bodily resurrection and metamorphosis from Caroline Walker Bynum. Her writings are grounded in historical scholarship, but offer a fresh perspective and a link to contemporary issues. Two of her books have been particularly helpful: *Metamorphosis and Identity* (New York: Zone Books, 2001); and *The Resurrection of the Body* (New York: Columbia University Press, 1995). Her comment on story is from p. 180 of *Metamorphosis and Identity*.

Chapter 4: Amazing Seeds

Bunny McBride, *Women of the Dawn* (Lincoln: University of Nebraska Press, 1999), 5.

Alice Sebold, *The Lovely Bones* (Boston: Little, Brown and Company, 2002), 320.

I am indebted to Janet Martin Soskice, "Resurrection and the New Jerusalem" in *The Resurrection: An Interdisciplinary Symposium on the Resurrection*, ed. Stephen Davis, Daniel Kendall, and Gerald O'Collins (Oxford: Oxford University Press, 1997), pp. 41–58, for insights on Paul's teaching about the temple.

The Jewish story is from Belden C. Lane, "Rabbinical Stories: A Primer on Theological Method," *The Christian Century* (December 16, 1981): 1307–8.

David Toolan, *At Home in the Cosmos* (Maryknoll, N.Y.: Orbis, 2001) connects the new cosmology with an Earth ethics, and also with an incarnational and sacramental faith.

The prayer of Teilhard de Chardin is from his *The Divine Milieu* (New York: Harper & Row, 1960), 89–90.

Chapter 5: Awareness

Heather McHugh, "From 20,000 Feet" in *Hinge & Sign: Poems, 1968–1993* (Hanover, N.H.: University Press of New England, 1994), 215.

Antonio Damasio, *The Feeling of What Happens: Body and Emotion in the Making of Consciousness* (Orlando, Fla.: Harcourt, 1999), 3–4, 28.

Andrew Newberg and Eugene D'Aquili, *Why God Won't Go Away: Brain Science and the Biology of Belief* (New York: Ballantine, 2001), especially pp. 1–10 and 142–72. See also their earlier book, *The Mystical Mind* (Minneapolis: Fortress, 1999).

A leading scholar from each tradition presents clear summaries of Hinduism and Buddhism in *Life After Death in World Religions*, ed. Harold Coward (Maryknoll, N.Y.: Orbis, 1997). In *Encountering God:*

A *Spiritual Journey from Bozeman to Banaras* (Boston: Beacon, 1993), Diana L. Eck provides a scholarly but readable presentation of Hinduism, especially for someone from a Christian background. Another helpful resource is Kenneth Kramer, *The Sacred Art of Dying: How World Religions Understand Death* (Mahwah, N.J.: Paulist, 1988).

The quotation from the Upanishads regarding Atman and Reality is from the Chandogya Upanishad 6.9.4, *The Thirteen Principal Upanishads*, 2nd ed., trans. Robert E. Hume (Oxford: Oxford University Press, 1931), 246; the translation of the prayer for immortality is from Diana L. Eck, *Encountering God*, 117.

The story "The Golden Eagle" is in Anthony de Mello, *The Song of the Bird* (Chicago: Loyola University Press, 1983), 120–21.

Hermann Hesse, *Siddhartha* (New York: New Directions, 1951), 110–11.

James Luguri, *To Make a World: One Hundred Haiku and One Waka* (Copyright: Peter Luguri, 1987), 11, 17.

Chapter 6: In the Company of Friends

Cynthia Bourgeault, *Mystical Hope: Trusting in the Mercy of God* (Boston: Cowley Publications, 2001), 82. This is a slim, accessible book that weaves together prayer, the new view of the universe, and hope for the present and future.

Oscar Hijuelos, *Mr. Ives' Christmas* (New York: HarperCollins, 1995), 8–12, 136–37.

Mary Oliver, "Sunrise" in *New and Selected Poems* (Boston: Beacon, 1992), 125–26.

The phrase "physics of intimacy" is from Dana Zohar, *The Quantum Self: Human Nature and Consciousness Defined by the New Physics* (New York: William Morrow, 1990), 145.

Catherine Keller helpfully explains relational conceptions of space and time in *From a Broken Web: Separation, Sexism, and Self* (Boston: Beacon, 1986), 240–52. See also Lee Smolin, *The Life of the Cosmos* (New York: Oxford University Press, 1997), 221; and Michael Serres,

Hermes: Literature, Science, Philosophy, ed. Josue V. Harari and David F. Bell (Baltimore: Johns Hopkins University Press, 1982), especially p. 75, where Serres uses the images of sheaf and bouquet to describe the new sense of time.

David Bohm, *Wholeness and the Implicate Order* (Boston: Routledge, 1980), especially pp. 14–16.

Luce Irigaray, *This Sex Which Is Not One*, trans. Catherine Porter (Ithaca, N.Y.: Cornell University Press, 1985), 217. See also her *Between East and West: From Singularity to Community*, trans. Stephen Pluhacek (New York: Columbia University Press, 2002).

C. S. Lewis, *A Grief Observed* (New York: Bantam, 1963), 61–62. Many who struggle to understand how faith fits with the loss of a loved one find that this book speaks directly to their experience.

The Joy Harjo reflections are found on p. 51 of *A Map to the Next World: Poems and Tales* (New York: W. W. Norton, 2000), 51.

Elizabeth A. Johnson, *Friends of God and Prophets: A Feminist Theological Reading of the Communion of Saints* (New York: Continuum, 1998).

Chapter 7: Kinds of Presence

Karl Rahner, "The Life of the Dead" in *Theological Investigations*, trans. Kevin Smyth (Baltimore: Helicon Press, 1966), iv, 353–54.

Anca Vlasopolos, *No Return Address* (New York: Columbia University Press, 2000), 213.

Characteristics of personal knowing are discussed in *Knowing and Being: Essays by Michael Polanyi*, ed. Marjorie Grene (Chicago: The University of Chicago Press, 1969); and Mary Field Belenky, Blythe McVicker Clinchy, Nancy Rule Goldberger, and Jull Mattuck Tarule, *Women's Ways of Knowing: The Development of Self, Voice, and Mind* (New York: Basic Books, 1986).

Rita Rainsford Rouner, "A Short While towards the Sun: Poems and Reflections on Continuity and Loss, after the Death of a Child" in *If I Should Die*, ed. Leroy S. Rouner (Indiana: University of Notre

Dame Press, 2001), 13–38. The poem "Into the Bright Immensities" is on p. 31.

Jürgen Moltmann uses the phrase "second presence" in "Is There Life after Death?" in *The End of the World and the Ends of God: Science and Theology on Eschatology*, ed. John Polkinghorne and Michael Welker (Harrisburg, Penn.: Trinity Press International, 2000), 238–55. See also Moltmann's *The Coming of God: Christian Eschatology* (Minneapolis: Fortress, 1996).

The meaning of presence in religion, philosophy, and interpersonal relations is distilled in Ralph Harper's brief book *On Presence: Variations and Reflections* (Philadelphia: Trinity Press International, 1991).

Vicky Galo and Janet Bristow of Hartford, Connecticut, are credited with starting the practice of knitting comfort shawls in 1998.

Chapter 8: One With the Universe

Mary Oliver, *The Leaf and the Cloud* (Cambridge, Mass.: Da Capo Press, 2000), 45.

Jane Goodall, *Reason For Hope: A Spiritual Journey* (New York: Warner Books, 1999), 173–74.

For Irenaeus, see Bernard McGinn, *The Foundations of Mysticism: Origins to the Fifth Century* (New York: Crossroad, 1991).

Fritjof Capra and David Steindl-Rast, *Belonging to the Universe: Explorations on the Frontiers of Science and Spirituality* (Harper San Francisco, 1991), 14–15.

The discussion and quotation from Rosemary Radford Ruether regarding the Matrix are in her *Gaia & God: An Ecofeminist Theology of Earth Healing* (San Franciso: Harper San Franciso, 1992), 247–53. In her book *The Quantum Self: Human Nature and Consciousness Defined by the New Physics* (New York: William Morrow, 1990), p. 142, Dana Zohar refers to the subatomic level of elementary particles, where there is no death in the sense of permanent loss, as the "well of eternity."

Teilhard de Chardin expressed on numerous occasions his conviction that union differentiates. See, for example, *The Phenomenon of Man*, trans. Bernard Wall (New York: Harper & Row, 1965), 262.

Marjorie Suchocki, *The Fall to Violence: Original Sin in Relational Theology* (New York: Continuum, 1994), 159.

Danah Zohar, *The Quantum Self: Human Nature and Consciousness Defined by the New Physics*, 141–53.

Barbara J. Scot, *The Stations of Still Creek* (San Francisco: Sierra Club, 1999), 181.

Joyce Fossen's poem is in *Earth Prayers from Around the World: 365 Prayers, Poems, and Invocations for Honoring the Earth*, ed. Elizabeth Roberts and Elias Amidon (San Franciso: Harper San Francisco, 1991), 30.

Chapter 9: Remembrance

Gerard Manley Hopkins, "The Leaden Echo and the Golden Echo" in *Poems and Prose of Gerard Manley Hopkins*, ed. W. H. Gardner (Baltimore: Penguin, 1953), 54.

Doris Grumbach, *The Pleasure of Their Company* (Boston: Beacon, 2000), 1–8.

Danah Zohar provides a helpful explanation of the meaning of memory in modern physics in *The Quantum Self: Human Nature and Consciousness Defined by the New Physics* (New York: William Morrow, 1990), 107–40.

Gail Tsukiyama, *The Samurai's Garden* (New York: St. Martin's Press, 1994), 180.

John O'Donohue introduces Celtic traditions, including prayers and blessings, in *Anam Cara: A Book of Celtic Wisdom* (New York: HarperCollins, 1997). See especially Chapter 6, "Death: The Horizon Is in the Well," pp. 199–231. See also Esther De Waal, *The Celtic Way of Prayer: The Recovery of the Religious Imagination* (New York: Doubleday, 1997).

In discussing Alfred North Whitehead's thought, I am working from his *Process and Reality*, corrected edition, ed. David Ray Griffin and Donald W. Sherburne (New York: Macmillan, 1978), 340–51. Helpful explanations of this aspect of Whitehead's thought are found in William A. Beardslee, *A House for Hope* (Philadelphia: Westminster, 1972); and Marjorie Hewitt Suchocki, *God, Christ, Church: A Practical Guide to Process Theology* (New York: Crossroad, 1982). David Ray Griffin provides a very complete introduction to Whitehead's philosophy in *Reenchantment without Supernaturalism: A Process Philosophy of Religion* (Ithaca, N.Y.: Cornell University Press, 2001). Griffin treats the question of Whitehead's belief in life after death on pp. 230–46.

Marilyn Nelson, "Cover Photograph" in *The Fields of Praise: New and Selected Poems* (Baton Rouge, La.: Louisiana State Press, 1997), 3. Nelson's sequence of poems, "Mama's Promises," from which this poem comes, pictures God as a nourishing, sometimes angry, but always loving, mother.

Chapter 10: Meeting the Light

J. Philip Newell, *The Book of Creation: An Introduction to Celtic Spirituality* (Mahwah, N.J.: Paulist, 1999), 4. Throughout the book Newell shows how the Celtic tradition finds God's image deep within all living beings.

On the Oglala practice of greeting the dawn, see *The Sixth Grandfather: Black Elk's Teachings Given to John G. Neihardt*, ed. Raymond J. DeMallie (Lincoln: University of Nebraska Press, 1984), 226.

Alexandra Morton describes the behavior of whales in *Listening to Whales: What the Orcas Have Taught Us* (New York: Ballantine, 2002).

Dante Alighieri, *The Divine Comedy*, trans. Charles S. Singleton (Princeton, N.J.: Princeton University Press, 1975), vol. I, *Inferno*, 5.28, 49.

Raymond A. Moody, *Life After Life: The Investigation of a Phenomenon — Survival of Bodily Death* (New York: Bantam, 1976).

I am indebted to the careful research that Carol Zaleski presents in her two books on near-death experiences. The longer and more detailed of these is *Otherworld Journeys: Accounts of Near-Death Experience in Medieval and Modern Times* (New York: Oxford University Press, 1987). A shorter book, which was first given as a set of lectures at the University of St. Mary of the Lake/Mundelein Seminary, is *The Life of the World to Come: Near-Death Experience and Christian Hope* (New York: Oxford University Press, 1996). My summary of the elements that characterize these experiences is adapted from *The Life of the World to Come*, p. 19. The two stories of light, and the account of the survivor of anaphylactic shock, are from *Otherworld Journeys*, pp. 5 and 21. Zaleski discusses the convergence of knowledge and love in near-death experiences on p. 125 of *Otherworld Journeys*.

Thomas Merton, *Conjectures of a Guilty Bystander* (New York: Doubleday, 1966), 140–42.

Dante Alighieri, *The Divine Comedy*, trans. Charles S. Singleton (Princeton, N.J.: Princeton University Press, 1975), vol. III, *Paradiso*, 381. An excellent analysis of the sources of Dante's thought is Peter S. Hawkins, *Dante's Testaments: Essays in Scriptural Imagination* (Stanford, Calif.: Stanford University Press, 1999).

Antoine de *Saint-Exupéry, The Little Prince*, trans. Katherine Woods (New York: Harcourt, Brace, & World, 1943), 85.

Chapter 11:
Earth Crammed With Heaven

Elizabeth Barrett Browning, *Aurora Leigh* 7:821–824, ed. Margaret Reynolds (Athens: Ohio University Press, 1992), 487.

Gerard Manley Hopkins, "God's Grandeur" in *Poems and Prose of Gerard Manley Hopkins*, ed. W. H. Gardner (Baltimore: Penguin, 1953), 27.

Jane Kenyon, "Peonies at Dusk" in *Otherwise: New and Selected Poems* (St. Paul, Minn.: Graywolf Press, 1996), 207.

Chet Raymo, *Natural Prayers* (St. Paul, Minn.: Hungry Mind Press, 1999), 129–32, 176–79.

Ursula Goodenough, *The Sacred Depths of Nature* (New York: Oxford University Press, 1998). Goodenough tells the story of the injured bird on p. 114.

Russell Stannard estimates this ratio of stars to humans while commenting on the size of the universe in *The God Experiment: Can Science Prove the Existence of God?* (Mahwah, N.J.: Hidden Spring, 2000), 104.

Brian Swimme, *The Hidden Heart of the Cosmos: Humanity and the New Story* (Maryknoll, N.Y.: Orbis, 1996), 46–49.

Jim Garvin is quoted in Kathy Sawyer, "A Mars Never Dreamed Of," *National Geographic* (February 2001): 37.

Paul Davies, *The Mind of God: The Scientific Basis for a Rational World* (New York: Simon & Schuster, 1992).

Christian DeDuve, *Vital Dust: Life As a Cosmic Imperative* (New York: HarperCollins, 1995), xviii. This position, in its various forms, is known as the Anthropic Principle, the precise and unlikely combination of circumstances required, from the moment of the Big Bang, to produce the human life we know. Some see it as suggesting design in the universe and a Designer who is the source of its purpose and meaning.

Dante Alighieri, *The Divine Comedy*, trans. Charles S. Singleton (Princeton, N.J.: Princeton University Press, 1975), vol. III, *Paradiso*, 343.

The Celtic blessings are from *Carmina Gadelica*, ed. Alexander Carmichael (Scottish Academic Press, 1976), III, 233, 215.

Chapter 12: The Mystery in Our Midst

Elizabeth Johnson makes her comment on love and the eternal in *Friends of God and Prophets: A Feminist Theological Reading of the Communion of Saints* (New York: Continuum, 1998), 194. Her entire book is a very clear and nuanced reflection on many aspects of life after death, but chapter 10, "The Darkness of Death," is especially helpful.

The story of the angel and the World Trade Center death was told on "Faith and Doubt at Ground Zero," a PBS *Frontline* special aired on September 3, 2002.

Peter L. Berger, *A Rumor of Angels: Modern Society and the Rediscovery of the Supernatural* (New York: Doubleday, 1970). See also *Angelic Spirituality: Medieval Perspectives on the Ways of Angels*, trans. Steven Chase (Mahwah, N.J.: Paulist, 2002). Karl Rahner talks about how God's grace already given to us is a basis for future hope in *Foundations of Christian Faith* (New York: Seabury, 1978), 103–4, 431–47.

I am grateful to Richard Viladesau, *Theology and the Arts: Encountering God through Music, Art and Rhetoric* (Mahwah, N.J.: Paulist, 2001) for expanding my understanding of beauty as a way to God, and for directing me to helpful resources.

Peter Shaffer, *Amadeus* (New York: Harper & Row, 1981), 18–19.

Boris Pasternak, *Doctor Zhivago*, trans. Max Hayward and Manya Harari (New York: New American Library, 1958), 44.

The selection from the paschal matins of the Orthodox Church is quoted in Miroslav Volf, *Exclusion and Embrace: A Theological Exploration of Identity, Otherness, and Reconciliation* (Nashville: Abingdon, 1996), 130.

Joy Harjo tells her story in *A Map to the Next World: Poems and Tales* (New York: W. W. Norton, 2000), 96.

William F. Lynch, *Images of Hope* (New York: New American Library, 1965) is a short classic on the topic of hope.

Gabriel Marcel, *The Mystery of Being*, trans. Rene Hague (Chicago: Henry Regnery, 1960), ii, 68. Some years ago, in his book *What Are They Saying About the Resurrection?* (New York: Paulist, 1978), Gerald O'Collins suggested that human experiences such as love and art could help us imagine the meaning of resurrection.

The Celtic prayer is from *Carmina Gadelica*, ed. Alexander Carmichael (Scottish Academic Press, 1976), iii, 53.

Chapter 13: Second Chances

The words of the Sufi mystic and poet Jelaluddin Rumi are from his poem "Say Yes Quickly" in *Open Secret: Versions of Rumi*, trans. John Moyne and Coleman Barks (Boston: Shambhala, 1984), 69.

Further discussion of the meaning of reincarnation in Hinduism and Buddhism can be found in *Life After Death in World Religions*, ed. Harold Coward (Maryknoll, N.Y.: Orbis, 1997); and Diana L. Eck, *Encountering God: A Spiritual Journey from Bozeman to Banaras* (Boston: Beacon, 1993). See also John Renard, *Responses to 101 Questions on Buddhism*, and *Responses to 101 Questions on Hinduism* (Mahwah, N.J.: Paulist, 1999).

Scientist Gary Zukav writes about evolution and reincarnation in a readable way in *The Seat of the Soul* (New York: Simon & Schuster, 1989). His earlier work, *The Dancing Wu Li Masters: An Overview of the New Physics* (New York: Simon & Schuster, 1979), is a helpful introduction to the contemporary worldview.

David L. Edwards presents insights on purgatory and hell in *After Death? Past Beliefs and Real Possibilities* (New York: Cassell, 1999).

For the material from Zora Neale Hurston, see *Their Eyes Were Watching God* (Chicago: University of Illinois Press, 1978), 138–39.

Gilbert K. Chesterton, "Beauty and the Beast," in *Orthodoxy* (New York: Doubleday, 1959), 50.

C. S. Lewis makes his suggestion regarding purgatory in *Reflections on the Psalms* (New York: Harcourt Brace, 1958), 8; and his caution on missing the experience of heaven in *Till We Have Faces: A Myth Retold* (New York: Harcourt Brace Jovanovich, 1956), 80–81.

Jonathan Schell speaks of nuclear holocaust as hell in *The Fate of the Earth* (New York: Alfred A. Knopf, 1982), 5.

The version of Psalm 1 is from Nan Merrill, *Psalms for Praying: An Invitation to Wholeness* (New York: Continuum, 2002), 1.

Chapter 14: Justice and Mercy

The translation of Psalm 23 is by Stephen Mitchell, *A Book of Psalms: Selected and Adapted from the Hebrew* (New York: HarperCollins, 1994), 12–13.

The story of the injured bicyclist is told in Michael Ko, "Pastor Describes Being Knocked Off Bike At Trial," *Seattle Times*, September 19, 2002, B3.

Jane Kenyon, "Notes from the Other Side" in *Otherwise: New and Selected Poems* (St. Paul, Minn.: Graywolf Press, 1996), 215.

There are many accounts of Julian of Norwich's life and thought. An introduction to her thought, and both the long and short texts of her writings, can be found in *Julian of Norwich: Showings*, trans. Edmund Colledge and James Walsh (New York: Paulist, 1978). Her reflections on the hazelnut, from chapter 5 of the long text, are on p. 183 of that volume. Another helpful presentation is Joan M. Nuth, *Wisdom's Daughter: The Theology of Julian of Norwich* (New York: Crossroad, 1991).

Wendy Farley explores the relationship between divine mercy and the problem of evil in *Tragic Vision and Divine Compassion: A Contemporary Theodicy* (Louisville, Ky.: Westminster/John Knox, 1990).

The Russian theoretical physicist Andrei Linde summarizes his theory regarding a self-reproducing inflationary universe in "Inflationary Cosmology and the Question of Teleology" in *Science and Religion: In Search of Cosmic Purpose*, ed. John F. Haught (Washington, D.C.: Georgetown University Press, 2000), 1–17. Linde suggests that our universe may have ballooned out of the space of a prior universe. It may be simply one of many more universes in a beginningless series, destined to collapse and then explode once more.

The contributors to *The End of the World and the Ends of God: Science and Theology on Eschatology*, ed. John Polkinghorne and Michael Welker (Harrisburg, Penn.: Trinity Press International, 2000) offer an excellent introduction to current issues. My summary of Walter Brueggemann's position is from his essay in that volume, "Faith at the Nullpunkt," 143–54.

Dermot A. Lane provides a comprehensive treatment of Christian themes related to the end-time, including a discussion of the eschatological dimensions of the Eucharist, in *Keeping Hope Alive: Stirrings in Christian Theology* (Mahwah, N.J.: Paulist, 1996).

The role of apocalyptic thought in the struggle for justice is explored in Wes Howard-Brooke and Anthony Gwyther, *Unveiling Empire: Reading Revelation Then and Now* (Maryknoll, N.Y.: Orbis, 1999). See also Ian Boxall, *Revelation: Vision and Insight. An Introduction to the Apocalypse* (New York: Pilgrim Press, 2002).

Judy Chicago, *The Dinner Party* (Garden City, N.Y.: Doubleday, 1979), 256.

Chapter 15: Walking With the Dying

Final Harvest: Emily Dickinson's Poems, ed. Thomas H. Johnson (Boston: Little, Brown and Company, 1961), 42.

The Tibetan Book of the Dead, trans. Robert A. F. Thurman (New York: Bantam, 1994).

Results of the 1997 Gallup Poll are summarized in "Life's End," *Society* 35 (March–April, 1998): 2.

Judith L. Lief, *Making Friends with Death: A Buddhist Guide to Encountering Mortality* (Boston: Shambhala, 2000). Buddhists talk about accompanying the dying in "Death As a Mirror: Caring for the Dying" in *Tricycle: The Buddhist Review* (Summer 2001): 29–43.

Also helpful is John Carmody, *Conversations with a Dying Friend* (Mahwah, N.J.: Paulist, 1992).

Maggie Callahan and Patricia Kelley, *Final Gifts: Understanding the Special Awareness, Needs, and Communications of the Dying* (New York: Bantam, 1993).

J. R. R. Tolkien, *The Lord of the Rings* (Boston: Houghton Mifflin, 1967), iii, 310.